SCRAPING PEGS

The Truth About Motorcycles

Michael Stewart

Beaten Stick Press

For Family and all the Angels of Mercy

CONTENTS

QUOTES

"The Road to Joy starts around the next bend."

MARTA, Volunteer

"It is a truth universally acknowledged, that a person in possession of a good fortune, must be in want of a motorcycle."

BOB, Motorcycle Friend

INTRODUCTION

The Truth About Motorcycles

Scraping Pegs
2022 Revision R1.1

Motorcycle Friends

I can't get Bob's death off my mind. It puzzles me. I hate conundrums. What the hell happened to Bob? The official cause of death? Drowning. Bob's bike flew into the Thompson River. It would make sense if Bob were racing his Ducati, but the cruiser? The cruiser never flew. It ambled. Bob loved to do both. As long as he wasn't under glass, tucked behind the locked-in clunk of a car door. Sometimes the sole of his boot scuffed the ground. "Touching down," he called it, with a silly grin planted on his face.

"Stupid," I called it. "You'll wear out your sole."

There were no shoe problems, broken bones, or significant physical damage—it was straightforward death-by-water. There Bob was, the wind all around him, but suddenly flying, an elegant soaring swan dive, with a sudden, shocking splash down into cold, swirling water and swimming. Or, probably, Not Swimming, or possibly Trying to Swim, since he drowned. There is no balance of power in the physics of trying to swim in swift water wearing heavy motorcycle boots. Force leans to the Lunar Rover Moonboots at the end of biker legs, winning the clawing-upwards-but-pulled-downwards battle. Not a bad way to go, though—at least he was motorcycling before he drowned. He was probably experiencing lingering JOY, not terror. Way better than just drowning. Is that the truth about motorcycling? That it embraces life and can even make dying better? Did Bob reach a state of euphoria and decide to take the next step? The ultimate test of man and machine. Typical Bob, leaving questions behind. There was more to him than met the eye, that's for sure. That's why we got along. Our voices and laughter were carried away by the wind. Singing. Crying. Cursing. On a motorcycle, you can say whatever you like. Bob and I never spoke much, but we said many things.

I remember we were at Tony's Deli when I told Bob about the time I nearly drowned in a river, dragged out inches before the Valley of Death. How to explain a near-death experience? "You had to be there," I ended up saying. Did Bob take me literally? Decide to see for himself? Who knows? Not me. Our relationship wasn't deep. Bob probably thought I was weird, talking about passing without being on-motorcycle. I don't think this explains what the hell happened to Bob. My friend would have sent a clue like, "going for a swim." He enjoyed being mysterious.

We laughed at the same jokes, enjoyed each other's company, and got along fine, but riding bonded us, not history. Our paths predominately crossed at prearranged events. We were Motorcycle Friends. More than acquaintances, but not good buddies, pals, or even chums. We hit it off, then shrugged. *Too busy and too damn difficult to make an effort in real life. It's easier on Facebook.* Why did we not spend more time together? When Bob was alive, it wasn't urgent. *One of these days, I'll make an effort.* I never bothered.

Now Bob's dead. No more thinking, *we should get together for coffee or something besides motorcycles*, and then, getting together with Bunny, my cat, instead. So, we'll stay cemented forever at biker friends. Now I'm stuck at Bob-less and will never know if there is something beyond biker friend. It's not like I have so many friends I couldn't have squeezed more Bob in. Like me, Bob was socially lazy, but I'm pathetically worse; he opened the door, which I never stepped through. It's a wonder I have any friends at all. Let alone a wife.

Bob was an experienced, excellent rider; he knew his way around motorcycles. A solid guy, the kind you want around if there's a flat tire or something that needs sorting out. Possibly not the most skilled swimmer, I guess? Don't have any idea as I said, we didn't know each other well. We weren't pals, and we sure never went to a beach or a motel pool together. Rode by a few on our bikes, though.

The police were equally confused but less interested in solving the conundrum than I was. "No evidence of road hazards," they reported. "Weather was fine, and there were no skid marks." *Did Bob do something stupid? Swerve to avoid a turtle? Experience mechanical failure?* He was anal about his machines—did it turn against him in a Terminator-like twist? Or did...

he... do something stupid?

The last time I saw Bob, I was the unwell one, lying in a bed at Royal Jubilee Hospital. My body was in for repair following a serious motorcycle accident. He visited; it was kind of a motorcycle event. "Wanted to get out for a ride," he said as if the hospital was on his route.

Bob's drop-by made me think, *when I'm able, I won't let things slip. I'll put more effort into life and friend-ships. Starting with Bob.* Hospital patients know: life changes in the blink of an eye. Get off your ass! Get on with it. Buy a new motorcycle! Absorb the rhythm of the Road to Joy. Don't put it off. Don't be a Motorcycle Dreamer.

"What type of screws do they use?" Bob wanted to know, referring to the orthopedic fasteners in the metal rods in my leg. "Philips or Robertson? Allen bolts?" I remember him guessing. "Stainless steel, I suppose?"

"Titanium, I think." I promised to check with the doctor. In hindsight, screws didn't strike me as some-thing a suicidal person would raise; then again, my mind was in Blobland when he came by. Trauma and powerful drugs will do that to you—I could easily have missed important clues. Could have ignored a pink gorilla climbing the wall next to me, for that matter. Or a slimy box jellyfish.

He had brought Kirkland Almonds with him in a sandwich bag, ranting that Costco had raised their price: "Jacked them up by a dollar ninety-five!" Al-monds weren't top of my mind then—they couldn't reach the top of my mind because they can't fly, and I was exploring the inner regions of the Outer Limits. To appear engaged, I asked, "Ever think about switching to walnuts, Bob? Fewer calories and more protein." Nope, Bob was a committed almond man. And not just any almonds, Kirkland Almonds. My nut knowledge seemed to fall flat, so I added, "but almonds taste way better." I appreciated Bob taking the time to put nuts in a sandwich bag for me, especially given the price increase. The cost of almonds was at most troubling. Certainly not deadly. I know Bob was close to doing a deal on a bike. Even the Costco price hike would not deny him his brand-new machine. He was in a strange almond rat hole, but I know he wasn't cheap. He especially enjoyed spending money on motorcycles.

Suicide rumors persist, driven by the need for an answer and Bob's placid demeanor. The police questioned me about his state of mind. It's false innuendo, I'm certain. "Ridiculous speculation. Bob was not that kind of guy." Or was he? Did I mention we weren't like brothers?

I always wanted to do a deep dive into the truth about motorcycling—understand what Bob had gleaned from years of riding. The MAGIC, JOY, and the drudgery we chatted about. But I hesitated. Never spit it out, as they say. Afraid Bob would hear an inappropriate question, given we weren't friends who shared deep thoughts. In the absence of Bob, and with no inkling about what happened to my could-have-been friend, I turned like billions of other mortals to the Oracle of Google and in supplication asked, "O Mighty

One—what then is the truth about motorcycles?" Having an off day, the Oracle replied, "Motorcycling is a society of rebels who refuse to live by mainstream laws and norms."

That's like saying, "Bob drowned." Cheap rhetoric. *Refuse to live by mainstream laws?* That's half the damn world—outlaw bikers, once the undisputed kings, have slipped down so far that financial advisers and animal trainers (among others) have usurped them. Veterinarians and florists ride Harleys and Triumphs. Are they refusing to live by mainstream laws and norms? The truth about motorcycles cannot be found in popular culture. Bob likely knew, but his thoughts were washed away. I

waited too long to ask my could-have-been friend. I must look elsewhere.

Zen and the Art of Motorcycle Maintenance

F ollowing the failure of The Sentient of Mountain View, California, to illuminate my darkness, I turned to a book that had left an impression on me years ago when I was susceptible: *Zen and the Art of Motorcycle Maintenance.* Back then, I filed it under "Profound." That seemed an excellent place to continue the search for truth. Why not take advantage of Mr. Pirsig's search for quality and the meaning of it all? To my young self, the book made me wonder, with deep phrases like Buddha lives in the circuitry of your motorcycle, whether these machines might be my pathway to finally getting answers? Such metaphysical concepts, linking motorcycles to God, surely will bring enlightenment. Had Mr. Pirsig figured things out? Or was I more gullible than suggestible?

I read the words, and as they sank in, I torqued bolts, checked valves, changed the oil, and in a dozen other ways, became one with my early motorcycles. In this unity of man and machine, engine vibrations spoke to me: I not only rode, but I also diagnosed. Arrhythmia, piston slap, pressure drops: my machines wordlessly conveyed their condition with every sound and unexpected gyration. I bought into the notion of a man-machine bond; after all, Buddha hangs out in inanimate objects, at least in the Lord of Machines, motorcycles. Would motorcycle maintenance illuminate my life?

No. It would not.

Forgotten, the book slipped behind me—we went our separate ways. I experienced moments of JOY from riding and some satisfaction from wrenching but did not achieve enlightenment while twisting bolts. I came to prefer Marta's simple logic: "Sometimes motorcycles suck and sometimes they don't."

Now, thanks to Bob, motorcycles and truth are constantly on my mind. So, with great expectation, I began to re-read the best-selling "motorcycle" book of all time, eager to reconnect with the potentialities of my youth. *Get ready to transform*, I promised myself as I opened the magical book. *I'm ready, Mr. Pirsig! Experienced. Enlighten me!*

It did not go well.

I turned my e-reader off at page fourteen. *Zen's* words were like choking down an overcooked, slimy, vile Brussels sprout. "Give it a chance," I said to encourage myself against quitting on page nine, but the expression, "There's no going back," is fact. My days of wonder had drained out of me. No longer Zen material, I had to accept, *Curmudgeonly Jackassism* is my guiding light. It doesn't demand followers find answers in weird old books. If the solution isn't in a two-minute YouTube video, forget it. Except for the truth about motorcycles and what happened to Bob, most necessary answers are on YouTube.

Rather than ponder the wonder of the philosopher's musings, my mind went numb–similar to the dull numbness that seeps up through the foot pegs on straight miles of nothingness just before Compliancy Swamp. "Screw this," Jackassism reminded me. I put my reader down and switched to YouTube. YouTube has better video explanations than books.

Decades of life changed me, long before I took up residence on the eleventh floor of Royal Jubilee hospital (my daughter works as an RN there, by the way. She's the #1 Angel of Mercy, that girl. Takes after her mother?). Life changes your filters. The words of Pirsig's story were the same; his message immutable. No, in facing the truth, I had to admit: it was I who had changed from a wide-eyed Zen Grasshopper wannabe to a mature, decrepit curmudgeon. I'd accepted reality, both Life, the Beautiful, and Life, the Bully.

Existence hardens people. Was Gandhi immune, I wonder? Was he able to remain perpetually childlike? Is it possible to withstand the force of time? Does Professor Hawking address this in his acclaimed book, *A Brief History of Time,* or is it too brief to examine the Gandhi-Time scrubbing away awe question and the truth about motorcycles?

In my mind, *Zen* was picked up by the librarian in "Profound" and handed to the janitor to recycle, who instead filed it under "Abstruse." Life happens; we begin full of wonder and open to possibilities and turn into Curmudgeonly Jackasses. The cure? Motorcycles.

What happened to me is what happens to every young adult, except maybe Mahatma Gandhi and Nelson Mandela? Or is that also a myth, like popular motorcycle culture? What is the truth about old Mr. Gandhi? I'll check YouTube.

The clock ticked. Time passed, and in its passing laid more of the cards of life on the table; a bigger picture showed: not as poetic or as delicately pretty as it once had been, though it was less desperate, not as urgent, now only mildly insistent. Nowadays, the good and bad of motorcycling share equal weight in my mind. The mundane balanced with the mystical. The JOY and the misery. "Sometimes motorcycles suck and sometimes they don't."

I prefer Marta to the *Zen* book.

"You take a handful of sand from the endless land-scape of awareness around us and call that handful of sand the world." *

"The Buddha, the Godhead, resides quite comfortably in the circuits of a digital computer or the gears of a cycle transmission as he does at the top of a mountain, or in the petals of a flower." *

*Robert M. Pirsig, Zen and the Art of Motorcycle Maintenance

Maybe people like Gandhi can hold on to statements like the ones above throughout their lives? They are soldiers. Strong. Steadfast, with resilient right brains. Fending off time as it scrubs away at "Profound." I accept that Mr. Pirsig's observations make as much sense as any other explanation of inexplicable things. Though after my older self reread those fourteen turgid pages, I still didn't have a clue about the really big questions, the kind the ancient Greek philosophers in Mr. Pirsig's book ponder with superlative ease: Aristotle nonchalantly wrestling elaborate theories as simply as Valentino Rossi guiding his Yamaha through a series of curves.

Horseshit, I thought as I reread *Zen,* but I don't get Aristotle either, and in serious corners, at times, I looked like an out-of-control SQUID (we'll review SQUIDs in a bit). I remained spiritually disconnected from the Cosmos but proximally connected to YouTube, my cat, Bunny, and my best friend, Pearl.

Modern motorcycles insist I remain disconnected. Today's two-wheelers bear little similarity to the 1966

Honda Super Hawk in the *Zen* book. No tinkering by amateur mechanics: please. No wave of Mr. Pirsig type, do-it-your-selfers, spiritually bonding to their machines, nursing them until their last breaths. Not smart business. Industry prefers the replace-not-repair philosophy. The art of motorcycle maintenance, tearing down a modern engine at the side of the road using the manufacturer's toolkit, with or without Buddha's guidance, is history. Now consumers are drawn in with lifestyle advertisements to bond profitably with the latest model. Safety enhancements like ABS reassure timid shoppers. That's the sensible, money-making approach reasonable business owners should follow. Zen has no place in the boardroom. Gandhi would have made a horrible CEO. *How about we all walk?* Give me a break! Even Buddha rides motorcycles, Mr. Gandhi. According to Mr. Pirsig.

Back to Bob momentarily. Bob experienced motorcycling JOY; the indescribable feeling riders occasionally revel in, sitting on two wheels (or three), slicing through air, uncaged. A phenomenon motorcyclists cherish. Bob's JOY ended in the Thompson River. Mine ended on Highway 20—you're going to have to wait for that story as well. It's crucial to mention JOY. Pegs is about Truth. "Truth," says Marta, "Can be pretty grim. But never lose sight of JOY."

Bike sellers: relax–I'm determined to make it back to your shop one of these days. May need my son's assistance. He's strong, kind, and level-headed (how does a jackass end up with two great kids?). I'll demand a sizable discount on your latest model. I love to ride. You do sell mobility scooters, don't you? Motor-cycle-to-scooter is a natural progression. "Sometimes via a motorless wheelchair rolled out of a drug treatment center," Marta pointed out.

To be fair, *Zen and the Art of Motorcycle Maintenance* isn't really about motorcycles or maintenance. Instead, it's about philosophy, exploring the mysteries of the unknown—a pie-in-the-sky, clever book for the right side of your brain (to differentiate, I call right side, Brain Brian). Brain Brian is creative and full of wonder. Left won't even peak at *Zen*; prefers Newton's *Mathematical Principles of Natural Philosophy*.

Marta nailed it: "sometimes truth isn't very profound. Ride, don't look for truth in books... Scraping Pegs, excluded."

John Prine

I favour bare-bones points of view these days—no gray or grey. Leave Plato and Socrates out of the mix. Let's tell it like it is, not flaunting our amazing motorcycle adventures, awesome relationships, and do-it-ourselves maintenance as a pathway to a higher level of consciousness. Just ride—discover the MAGIC in your machine; it leads to JOY. Riders know stereotypes and popular culture do not define motorcycling. Instead, cut to the chase, like singer-songwriter John Prine who offers common-sense advice in many of his songs. You can find some of them on YouTube, of course.

So, here's the deal with this book series: it's the John Prine of motorcycling. Rest in peace, John. *It is what it is, and it ain't what it ain't.* I can't argue with his logic. It is Truth. I like his songs; they keep me pointed in the right direction, unlike *Zen and the Art of Motorcycle Maintenance*, which is like political science, the science of theater.

Put *Scraping Pegs* aside and read *Zen* if you want the esoteric world. If you're looking for a technical riding manual, or the drama of life as a bad boy or mama biker, or globe-trotting rides to far-off lands, this book isn't it. We're exploring the truth about motorcycles. We're trying to discover what happened to Bob?

The reality is that crappy weather, careless drivers, sore asses, flat tires, death, and other aggravations creep into both life and riding. I haven't morphed into a stereotypical biker dude despite years in the saddle. I'm just a jackass, probably a lot like you. My truth is: a motorcycle put me in a bed at Royal Jubilee Hospital. But I did discover JOY on-motorcycle. It can be elusive, but it's there. It's why we ride, so I may buy another, if I'm able because:

Truth About Motorcycles: you must have a bike to find JOY.

Press an experienced rider, and they'll admit to horrible days, mechanical disasters, soured relationships, and bad attitudes. "Like life, don't you think," Marta asks? Some, like my cousin Lenny, will show you their wounds. Then they'll step back and add, without a hint of irony, "The worst rides make the best stories." Motorcycling memories are always rosier in the rear-view mirror. Maybe that's the Zen of it?

In Marta's reality, "Motorcycle culture is sprinkled with pixie dust." But now riders have *Pegs*, a down-to-earth, tell-it-like-it-is book, or series of books because, unlike the cosmos or Newtonian physics, motorcycling can't be straightened out in a single volume or a couple of YouTube minutes—it's far too complex. If it were straightforward, we'd understand what the hell happened to Bob.

Motorcycles

Because Pegs is non-fiction (albeit creative), clarifications are necessary to preserve integrity. To start, as you go through the pages, understand that the use of "motorcycling" in this book refers to the western recreational use of the machine. Millions of people ride Transport Bikes to help sustain their lives, knowing full well that riding can be neither glamorous nor mystical. Marta guffaws uncontrollably at the thought of Transport Bikers reading *Zen and the Art of Motorcycle Maintenance.* Enjoy the book as a work of western absurdism if you're in that category. I hope you find Life, the Beautiful in your way.

Also, know *Scraping Pegs* holds no brand or style sacred. We're talking motorcycles, not marketing hype or personal preference, so don't get your knickers in a knot because *Pegs* doesn't drone on about your favorite machine.

Motorcycles are like music. Tastes change over time, from nursery rhymes to country, to heavy metal, and so on. A category or two is skipped along the way, like Gregorian chants or Fat Bob custom choppers, but an evolutionary path exists. Who wants a lifetime of being stuck in a rut? How many drum solos can one listen to before knowing it's time to move on? No matter your two-wheel preference, you're welcome here.

Confession: I've lived through periods of motorcycle bigotry. I'm not Motorcycle Gandhi. Today I'm close to agnostic (a severe accident will change your perspective). Admittedly, I'm developing a preference for a particular mobility scooter brand.

I've switched indiscriminately and, often foolishly, between many types and brands of motorcycles. Owned them all, or knew someone who owned one, or saw one driving down the street, somewhere, sometime. Possibly. I can't remember for sure. Bob might know if the industry makes a Therapy Bike, but he's dead.

Don't own a motorcycle? No problem–the logic within *Pegs* can be applied, with some alteration, to trout fishing or any undertaking. You must do a bit of mental juggling, but it is sortable. I've tested adaptability by applying the Rules to crossing the street in a wheelchair—it worked great. I almost got run over once, but I squeaked across in one piece thanks to Awareness (part of having a Motorcycle State of Mind). It'll be invaluable when I'm ripping around on a mobility scooter.

We ride (or cross streets) because it presents possibilities. *It is what it is and it ain't what it ain't* and that's okay, Mr. Pirsig. No need to ramble on in search of cosmic answers. Marta suggests you should have told yourself this when you started pondering, "Get a grip."

Motorcycle Riding Rules

I follow ten Motorcycle Riding Rules (MRR). Keep them in my back pocket. Even though I'm not riding now, they're there and are easy to adapt for use when not on-motorcycle. I made them up myself, gradually over time, as experience taught me her lessons. They're somewhat metaphysical, not black and white like the safety rules you learn in Parking Lot Cone School. They'll help you accept the Truth About Motorcycles, but you'll have to do some THINKING on your own—this isn't YouTube.

If you're good at adapting things, save money by avoiding the cost of a separate *How to Live A Perfect Life* book. Tons of people on YouTube have answers and are keen to sell you theirs (you only get the first rule free. After that, you can purchase a subscription, pay up front, or watch lots of ads). Save time and money by applying MRR instead. No sense shelling out for stuff like, "Befriend people who want the best for you." How the hell are you supposed to do that? How do you tell who wants to do the best for you? People don't come with product specifications and warning labels like machines. Plus, what if you're socially lazy, like me? "There's a lot of bullshit on You-Tube," Marta says.

"Answers too," I said, but she's right.

It might sound like a copout, but studying the Rules alone isn't enough. That's why you won't find MRR on YouTube. To be effective, you must do some heavy lifting. Read the Rules, Think, Tailor, and work at Embedding them in your own way. It's all up to you. *Pegs* isn't pixie dust. Buddha traveled to the Bodhi tree, by the Mahabodhi temple, to find His enlightenment. He didn't sit on His holy ass, waiting for YouTube to come along and tell Him what to do. Bandwidth was slow in His day, and tablets were stone. You must also take a journey, make an effort. And be lucky (sorry, but it's about Truth, remember)?

If you want the condensed version, the Rules are mostly about Awareness, Ability, and Accountability. That's it. I'll share them with you. Hopefully, they'll help you develop, or reinforce, a Motorcycle State of Mind. It's not deep. Of course, Life is simply about Breathing and Eating.

God didn't turn over every rock in His list of ten commandments. By the way, one of the original commandments is incomplete. Thou Shall Not Covet Thy Neighbor's Goods. What if your neighbor parked the **Motorcycle of Your Dreams** beside your It'll Do Bike with its flat tire and leaky fork? Know that God does not condemn all motorcyclists to eternal damnation and Hell. Do not covet the glorious creature sitting on the motorcycle, but the bike itself is what theologians call "an ipso facto clarification of the rule." Scholars cite Perfect Creation to substantiate this modern-day interpretation: Thou Shall Not Covet Thy Neighbor's Goods, Except for Motorcycles (two thousand years from Jesus). Some theologians talk about how motorcycles represent the second coming of Christ, it's a disputed theory like a lot of other stuff in the good books.

For many years I was lucky. Then I crashed. I'll share that story. I don't want *Pegs* to be purely academic. To be honest, even Left Brain found *Mathematical Principles of Natural Philosophy* to be a bit dry, a little over the top with its laws and theorems. Good for mopping up spills, though. Its dryness could use some humanity and JOY for sure. Just because my gullibility has eroded and I've fallen into Curmudgeonly Jackassism, doesn't mean I've turned to stone, without feelings, lacking empathy, utterly devoid of spiritualism. I live with Bunny, a cat, for Heaven's sake. Also, a dog, Pearly. Cats and dogs often speak the Truth. I like to run things by them. Too bad they don't ride. I'd love to ride with Bunny and Pearl; especially now I can no longer tag along with Bob.

Bob owned a cat, Trident. Trident passed of old age. Bob wouldn't have flown into the Thompson River if Trident was alive. He loved his cat. Almost as much as his motorcycles.

You must absorb all ten Motorcycle Riding Rules, so please stick with me through the Rules part of *Pegs*, even though it may be a bit of a grind, or you may be a know-it-all, like me, and want to skip ahead. I promise there will be a crash if you persist. Do doctors and engineers call it quits part way through their studies? *Good enough! I'm ready to drill into a cerebellum or re-engineer the Space Station guidance system. Hand me that duct tape and the hammer drill! Where's my certificate? And my Lunar Rover Moonboots?* No! They have what we call "professional standards." I want you to be a motorcycle professional.

For Bob.

Kickstands Up!

PART 1: THE DESERT

RULE #1,
EVERYONE

F riends said to me: "You're a sitting duck on that thing. It's just a matter of time before someone picks you off." On a motorcycle, you're a duck at a carnival sideshow. Poor ducks, nailed down, crucified at the back of a dumpy booth, powerless to educate themselves. Without protective gear, their survival is dependent on dumb luck and poor aim. Round and round they go, hoping Deadeye Dick (alias Dick, Double D [although he doesn't like that one so much] or Dicky to his friends) doesn't buy another ticket, step up with his sniper school gold medal pinned to his chest, and wreak carnage on the flock.

Kind of like motorcycles going around the streets. Cars and trucks (cagers) targeting bikes. Remember, it's a jungle out there, so here's Motorcycle Riding Rule #1—take it to heart, and you may spot Mr. Dick before he sets his crosshairs on your bike and pulls the trigger:

Rule #1: Everyone Is Trying To Kill You.

Climb on a motorcycle and you're in a war. Sure, it's

dramatic license until a nightmarish accident crushes carnival mascots turning them to roadkill.

There are no Rule terms and conditions—please add any if, therefores, and not-with-standings you see fit. Lawyers and psychologists love loosely written statements like Rule #1—they call them "major revenue streams."

"That *Pegs* book depressed the hell out of me, Doc. Just as I suspected for years, everyone is trying to kill me! Finally, it's all laid out here in *Pegs*! Black and white. Solid, irrefutable proof. I'm not 'loopy' like you say. Who's the nutcase now, Doc? It's not 'all in my head.' And I've caught glimpses of that sniper character stalking me!"

"Do you ride a motorcycle?"

"Huh?"

"I repeat, do you ride a motorcycle? How about a scooter?"

"No."

"Rule #1 only applies when you're *on-motorcycle*. You're not going to die. It's all here in this twelve-pager from the Beaten Stick Books lawyers. Only motorcyclists are sitting ducks. Hope that clears things up for you. Pay Gladys on your way out. Maybe take a nap when you get home. And book another set of appointments. You're still loopy and will require years of therapy."

Rule #1 is not to be used to validate *Chicken Little, the Sky is Falling,* delusions. Understand that the Motorcycle Riding Rules apply to, well, Motorcycling. Not trout fishing, practicing Ashtanga yoga, picking your nose, or other off-motorcycle activities. To be literally correct, #1 should read: *Only During the Time You Ride on a Motorcycle, Are You a Sitting Duck, and Therefore Everyone Will Try to Kill You.*

If you choose to adapt the Rules for use with off-motorcycle activities, do so with complete freedom, but be sure to make appropriate adjustments, add disclaimers, and revise the name. Don't confuse the Trout Fishing Rules (TFR) you'll use at Samson's Trout Fishing and Ice Cream Emporium with MRR or vice versa. For those keen on adaptation, TFR, Rule #1, for example, could be something like this: Everyone Will Figuratively Kill Me if I Don't Bring Home a Few Cutthroats or Dolly Vardens. The rule must help you concentrate on killing fish rather than dicking around with your lure collection. Do you see how each activity has its rule validation? Don't be afraid to adapt. *Pegs* is meant to be practical, not like the maintenance information in the *Zen* book, which is pathetically useless.

Pay attention to "Everyone." Take the case of my Auntie Minnie and her cute nephew, my cousin Lenny. He could do no wrong until, at fourteen, racing around in his shorts and flip-flops on his friend's minibike, Len ran over Elly, Auntie's cherished poodle. The beloved pet had to be put down. One night, five years later, while coming through an intersection on a green light, an SUV making a left turn clobbered Len's blue Yamaha 500. It ripped most of my cousin's right leg off—the driver: Auntie Minnie.

"The sun was in my eyes at that time of the evening," she swore in her police statement, which the police found credible: motorcycles are often invisible; it's common knowledge in the accident reconstruction business. They decided she was not on a vendetta against her nephew, harbouring a grudge over the death of her cherished pet. "We chalked it down to just another car-on-invisible-motorcycle incident," the investigating officer explained to his wife over dessert that night, a box of low-fat jelly donuts. "Happens all the time. Motorcyclists are sitting ducks. That's the fact of the matter."

Lenny really should have been thinking, *every time I fire up my Yamaha, everyone, including Auntie Minnie, will be trying to kill me.* It might have saved his leg, though the weathered stub is a conversation piece now. Stumpy likes to show it off at family gatherings. Bounces a sponge ball off of it. Always makes me think —should have taken up soccer/football instead of buying a bike. But I'm glad Stumpy has made good use of the two years he spent as a punk-ass biker. He told me, *Born to Be Wild,* was blaring on his speakers at the time of the crash. *Feel Like I'm Fixin' to Die* would have been more appropriate because Len never fully absorbed Rule #1. It's like being on the battlefield and thinking, *Come on, no one's going to try to kill me.*

Less conversationally brilliant is a neighbour I once had a crush on, sweet Mary McGregor. She was ravenous, drop-dead, glorious. Marta suspects Mary had a Wonder Woman, I'm invincible, perception of herself. No need to pay attention to #1. It's for everyone else. I have ageless beauty and therefore am immortal. Mary swerved to miss a distracted driver on Durance Lake Road. The rear wheel lost traction, skidded, then flipped Mary over the handlebars. Highsider, it's called. Too pretty to wear a helmet—she's brain-dead now though, the rest of her, the parts I was interested in as a young lad, were fine for years after the accident. Now Mary lives in Motorcycle Misery in the town of Numbskull.

Granted, the kid on the Grom really is dead, but only because old Dr. Farnsworth had a heart attack and blitzed him with his 4x4. Took the kid by complete surprise. Tidler Kid was wearing an approved helmet, but it didn't prevent brain bleed. Clearly, the good doctor was not intentionally trying to kill anyone. Nevertheless, Tidler Kid is dead. He was on-motorcycle and, therefore, a sitting duck. Dr. Farnsworth is also dead—the accident heart attack was the first of a few until his name came up in the Death Lottery (more on lotteries when we get to Rule #8).

Rule #1 is foundational. On a beautiful, peaceful day, it's easy to forget. Life can be a bully.

Many of us say, "Don't need to read the stupid instructions." Don't carry your outlaw attitude over from furniture assembly to motorcycle riding. IKEA cabinets can be aggravating, but a Swede will not pop out of the box and blow your head off if you lose a screw. You can always return your mistake to the store and grab some meatballs. If you're an I Don't Read Instructions Guy or Gal, understand DD does not park outside IKEA with his sniper rifle unless there's a bike in the lot.

Riders who choose not to develop a Motorcycle State of Mind are easy to pick off. Let's call these riders Blockheads. They're easy to spot. Deadeye sits behind them with a claw hammer. "Leave them be... many will kill themselves," Dicky told his brother, Radical. "Why waste a bullet? Use the hammer to finish them off."

There's death amongst the freedom and adventure on the open road and dirt tracks. Blockhead deaths, featured on the evening news, spotlight the certainty of Rule #1, which may benefit others. Bikers pay attention—time to get serious about safety. A prospective recruit buys a fishing rod instead of the second-hand two-wheel Killer Bike they had their eye on—lives are saved. It's heartening to know one motorcycle death can prevent another. Isn't that the theory of war? Kill to prevent others from being killed? Kill until the math works and peace descends on the land. Isn't it always about the math? Too much of this. Not enough of that. Let's have a war to divvy things up somewhat better. More for me. Less for you. Every time you climb on a motorcycle, you're going to war, and everyone will try to kill you. "Especially cagers with cell phones," Marta says.

Education is the best defense against #1. I like to compare motorcycle education with teaching myself how to stay healthy. Take nutrition classes: if you understand dietary guidelines, then disease and the relentless attack of aging have a fight on their hands. Incorporate other tools, like medical science and tuned-up neurotransmitters, and your defense grows stronger. Exercise! Get those muscles pumping. Eat some kale or enjoy a Brussels sprout smoothie if you're Flemish and starving. Swimming lessons are worth the effort, right? An insurance policy to keep you afloat when the tidal rip catches you, though, with a bit of luck, a gorgeous lifeguard will come to your rescue.

Motorcycle training is more complicated. Technical skills need honing and best practice tips such as *Ride Predictably, not like a jackass*, need remembering. This one also: *Worry more about getting killed than looking good on your bike. Wear high-visibility gear and those boots that make you look like you just stepped off the Lunar Rover.*

It's way more than simply going to Parking Lot Cone School and nodding. *Yeah, I know all about the idiots behind the wheel who will try to kill me.* Remember, there are another nine rules to help you avoid driving like a Blockhead—survival requires constant effort. You must put your back into it. MRR will guide you away from death and injury, improve your odds of not getting killed, but I'm obligated to state: *there is no guarantee.* Even the star student at Parking Lot Cone School needs luck. Her top marks won't help when a distracted driver triggers a chain of events that ends with her, well.... ending. Or at the very least, wishing she had bought a transit pass and stuck it out on the Number Ten bus. *So, what if it's always late and there's never a seat? At least no one's trying to kill me.* All the knowledge in the world won't help when you're that duck, just a'sittin' and a'mindin' your own business while Dick draws a bead. So, there's a saying, it's a question of when, not if, a rider will go down.

"Horseshit," I used to say. "Never happen to me."

But it did.

Despite Rule #1, it's not all doom and gloom. On the bright side, not riding is not a panacea. My friend Larry was a middle-aged organic broccoli-sprout-eating entrepreneur who refused to own a motorcycle. Despite the anti-motorcycle strike against him, we were firm friends. He knew more about health than I ever will, knew how not to be a sitting duck, and wouldn't even get on the back of my bike, saying, "I don't want to die." Now he's as dead as Bob. Lar choked on a seaweed cracker. An organic weed killed him; can you believe it? Even eating rolls the dice, so go ahead and ride!

Rejoice!

Truth About Motorcycle: JOY is not found in seaweed crackers. You must be on-motorcycle.

How about TV's Dr. Lean and Green, the nutritionist sales gal? Oh, yes, and Katarina Horvath, the fitness fanatic? Both are dead. Neither one owned a motorcycle. Their knowledge of fitness and nutrition didn't earn them a free pass, and you won't get one with motorcycle training because even educated ducks die. With ferocious frequency, Deadeye picks them off. It's his job, and he's very good at it. Sometimes his brother

Radical Dick helps out.

Some perspective: germs, sugar, bacon, greenhouse gas, your partner, water, sex, and many other things are trying to kill you, not just motorcycles. As humans know, the grim reality of existing is, is well... not existing. If you're an animal, not so daunting; they live in blissful ignorance. My cat, Bunny, is always carefree and relaxed. I think cats must have permanent Motorcycle Mindfulness, an attribute of JOY. Me, I have to go for a ride to clear my head.

Water hasn't killed me yet; crackers, neither. Nor motorcycling. Nor boredom. My time will come; my number will be called, but it won't be because I was a Blockhead.

Like most things, motorcycling has a back door. I tripped and fell through it. Soft landing, nothing broken. I wasn't intentionally trying to skirt the system or give society's laws and norms the biker salute.

I never completed a formal riding course or wrote a meaningful licensing test. I'll say more about how I slipped in shortly, but know that, though I'm undoubtedly cantankerous and stubborn, I am not a rebel—standing up for a worthy cause demands commitment and work, two of the things I ride to escape.

I was not born destined to become a Valentino Rossi. I had to work at developing a Motorcycle State of Mind. My training was purely coincidental. Luckily

Rule #1 was drilled by my mentor from the get-go, who assumed if I had that one rule in my back pocket, it'd buy me time to develop Ability and Awareness. It worked! Here I am in Royal Jubilee Hospital.

My back door was a desert in the Middle East. Quite a few Double D's lurking in the shadows. Scary looking; when you're young, folks decked out in unconventional dress, speaking a strange language, often glaring, are menacing until you learn, most are not. But some are.

Deserts appear to be bleak, no-man's lands, when you drive by, sealed inside a car. The land is a vast, beautiful canvass on foot, atop a camel, or riding a dirt bike. First, I trained on hard-packed sand on the city outskirts; soon, I graduated to hard-packed traffic in the city. Progression is swift when you're young; fear and caution is suppressed by naivety. Out I went into my version of Parking Lot Cone School: chaotic, undisciplined with thousands of riders on mopeds clogging streets already stuffed with taxis, cars, trucks, and diesel buses belching fumes. Throw in the odd donkey, a sprinkle of camels and some rangy goats or lambs with shackled legs (later, I might spot one of the lambs hanging in front of a house, freshly slaughtered, its blood draining into the ditch. Kabobs, I thought. Is it lunchtime?).

Pour in thousands of jaywalkers playing Frogger, and you have a large, polluted, congested city where Rule #1 is on steroids. A less-than-perfect student driver environment, western professionals, would say. There was no doubt my friend's advice was accurate; "Everyone will be trying to kill you!" Death was in plain sight; many of the toothless, foreboding-looking figures seemed eager to execute me. Killers were everywhere, not like driving in Porto, Edinburgh, Osaka, or Omaha. I had to learn quick or die trying.

Killers are on all roads, EVERYWHERE, not just the Middle East. There's no asterisk on Rule #1, *Except as listed on the *Peaceful & Safe Locations* website. Dedication to mastering the killing varies from place to place, but the rule includes "everyone," for a reason. Calm and orderly can fool you. Complacency will kill you. Spaniards, Scots, Japanese, and Arabs are all trying to kill you just as much as Nebraskan farmers, the Gandhi-like Jain followers in India, and the Juggalos in Ottawa suburbs.

I will grant you, in the interests of fairness, that these "killers" do not have a conscious desire for your death, nor do they drive Stephen King-like Christine mobiles fueled by insatiable blood-lust rather than gasoline. No, it's much more sedate. This fact may comfort you as you crawl up the bank. The Volvo left you and your battered bike sprawled in the ditch on its way home from the Festival of Peace, Light, and Harmony. The occupants' faint conversation heard on the breeze as it sped away:

"Oh, did anybody notice that bumping noise?"

"Think you clipped a cone, or maybe a turtle crossing the road, Mum."

"Ah, poor little thing... Are our peace and harmony souvenirs in the back okay, Son?"

"Yes, Mum, they are, and hey, look: there's that nice

Mr. Dick. Showed me his gun once."

After I left the Middle East, I occasionally provided technical support to risk lawyers—that is, lawyers who specialize in reducing the odds of something happening. More accurately, it should be known as the Specialization of Sucking the Joy Out of Life. Western governments are awash in it, which explains why the people-in-charge have no time for bikers. *Plus, few of them vote.* I can summarize the lawyers' views as:

1. enjoying life is risky, so don't;
2. there's good money to be made advising bureaucracies on ways to strip all enjoyment out of products and services;
3. at a minimum, add a six-page warning preamble to all product manuals;
4. always wear expensive business attire;
5. frown a lot when the words "carefree" and "personal responsibility" are mentioned.

 We shared a few motorcycle discussions. In fairness, we agreed on this point: everyone is trying to kill bikers. They showed me their handbook on safety. I stopped reading at *Everyone, Everywhere, All the Time is trying to Kill Everyone. Your safest bet is to buy a tank and drive at a safe pace—walking speed is suggested, stationary is ideal. Motorcycle owners should sit on their machines in the garage. With the en-*

gine off. By sit, we mean not on the bike but the floor in case the bike falls over. Sit far enough away from the motorcycle that if it falls over, it won't nail you. Even in your garage, keep an eye out for lightning, floods, snakes, loose electrical cables, box jellyfish, zombies and/or invading aliens. Intruding biker-outlaws attempting to lure you onto your bike is the supreme threat. Keep a shotgun handy for defence against these monsters. By handy, we mean triple-locked in a safe, secure cabinet with appropriate paperwork.

Of course, I couldn't help pointing out, "You can die eating a seaweed cracker as well."

They'd shoot me their, *nobody likes a smart-ass who doesn't take risk super-seriously*, glare. I was rescheduled to make room for "cereal box warning label" meetings. Fine by me., I didn't want risk mitigation setting me off on a rampage like in the movie *Machete*.

Valid as their recommendations are, the risk folks fail to see the actual point: that of Life itself. *Carpe Diem* and all that. Thank the Heavens, there will always be the subset of riders with over-blown confidence who will twist the throttle despite the prevalence of shit-happens Volvo drivers, road hazards, Blockheads, and their own inevitable demise.

But that is what it means to be human. Wet blankets muttering from the sidelines won't put an end to cornering faster than a fully loaded hay truck, the global standard endorsed by highway safety councils worldwide—a measure the government bureau of Risk Mitigation and Motorcycle Control would love to see lowered to zero.

It's horseshit!

Overtake that dawdling hay truck! Don't just over-take it: hold up your motorcycle training certificate, stand on your foot pegs and proudly yell: "I have a chance. I understand Rule #1. It's real. I intend to learn all ten rules!" If you're in one of those jurisdictions that have outlawed standing due to risk, do it anyway. Fuck it! Be an outlaw! Eat a cracker. Don't bow down to the wet blankets in the risk department! You're a motorcyclist who doesn't follow society's norms. So, give them the biker salute.

Scrape Your Damn Pegs!

Then sit down, jam that accelerator open, bear down in the corner and lean until sparks fly. Cover your ears, my legal friends. The truth about motor-cycles and life is, both are risky. But, as you say, "Fortu-nately, there is damn good money in it."

RULE #2, YOU

A large, well-respected study found that 25% of motorcycle accidents involve a single vehicle and no inanimate objects. Be it Blockheads gunning down empty roads, on MV Augusta's at two in the morning, or middle-aged moms and dads, enjoying their third ever ride on a peaceful Sunday afternoon. YOU can be your own worst enemy.

Rule #2: Don't Kill Yourself By Doing Something Stupid!

Yes, included in the "Everyone" of Rule #1 is... you. It's not just Auntie Minnie and Dr. Farnsworth stirring the pot or other NimRods (cagers who can't comprehend motorcycles) who are to blame. It's YOU. Be Accountable! Much of the time it's STUPID YOU! 'Stupid' is a pervasive human trait, and as the saying goes: *You can't fix stupid.* Well, maybe yes, maybe not, but at the very least Rule #2 will help you recognize foolish behavior, which may save your ass.

Everyone can be STUPID, even Mr. Gandhi. *I prefer always to walk, never to ride*—stupid! Ask Mr. Google or Mr. Pirsig; it's well known that *on-motorcycle* is the path to enlightenment or at least uncaged free-floating thought. Walking not balanced with riding is stupid, Mr. Gandhi.

My risk lawyering friends add their safety pre-ambles to product manuals in an attempt to prevent stupid, but we're all too weak in the head to read them. Kidding! The warnings are there to defend clients against litigation. No one cares if you read them or not, as long as you check the little box that says you did. Stupid! MRR doesn't have a preamble or a *Read and Agree* box. You consent to put your life on the line when you climb on.

Do you think Rule #2 is so obvious, it shouldn't be a rule? It's common sense and shouldn't be a rule. It's nonsensical how uncommon common sense is, isn't it? Especially when you're young and driving a V-Rod.

What's evident to you might not be to me, but you probably didn't fall through a back door? I didn't get all the facts quickly. I was what they call a "slow two-wheeler." The Motorcycle Riding Rules came to me over many years. Instead of Parking Lot Cone School, I went to the School of Fly by the Seat of Your Pants while trying not to do something stupid. All intelligent people start STUPID.

I had to roll up my sleeves to learn the rules. Not like that other guy who also got a set of ten rules. We're told Moses went up Mount Sinai—what we're not told is he undoubtedly rode the Holy Dirt Bike. God didn't want to hang around while Moses struggled up the mountain in ratty, homemade sandals. That would be STUPID! Why linger when He knows about Hill Climb JOY? At the top, boom went the lightning strike. One-minute humanity is rudderless;

the next, Ten Commandments! On the original tablet, with a 1 foot by 2-foot screen—one for him, one for Sarah, so there was no arguing over who would read what and when. I wasn't there, but I'm sure God also practiced risk mitigation and gave Moses' saddlebags to bring the tablets down the mountain safely. "Don't be STUPID, Moses. Feather the brake." No Lunar Rover Moonboots to replace his crappy sandals, though. "Remember Moses," God said. "Everyone will be trying to kill you." Kidding – that was Marta being a Smart Alec, but it seems Everyone was trying to kill the Son of God. If only Moses hadn't driven the Holy Dirt Bike into the Dead Sea.

Moses received the Rules for all Humanity; I made mine for myself and a few adopters. I wrote them on a notepad and then laboriously typed them into my tablet so they'd be easy to share. I'm not God, but let's face it, writing the Ten Commandments in stone made going viral impossible and left home base wide open for competing doctrines. I don't want to risk calling it STUPID, but it certainly wasn't media-friendly.

I practice Curmudgeonly Jackassism; we're not a profoundly religious bunch. However, I have a hallowed belief that my first motorcycle, a Suzuki TS-125, was a direct descendent of the Moses Mount Sinai dirt bike. An altar to remember a holy event. It'll all be revealed when they stumble on The Motorcycle Testament. Moses and I have shared the feeling of scraping pegs and defying gravity as it tries to pull down but rises to where God is. The Holy Father of Motorcycle JOY.

It's worth considering the fact that, had life been encumbered by risk management in the year 1300 BC, Moses would have kept God waiting while the Holy Lands Risk Department debated the danger of ascending Mount Sinai. Then another long delay while each Commandment got a minimum six-page cautionary warning preamble and God disclaimer. Come to think of it, religion has its own Rule #1: Every Mainstream Religion is Trying to Kill Every Other Mainstream Religion. Maybe not? I don't know. Did I mention I'm not deeply religious? But from watching TV news, it sure seems like it could be a rule?

God's rule, "Thou Shall Not Kill", is explicit. It means "Do Not Kill Dead." D.E.A.D. Finito! For both MRR Rule #1 and Rule #2, "Kill" is more generic, a cover-all term, not limited to its use in Deadeye's sniper training manual or on ancient slabs of stone commandments. In MRR, we extend kill to include injured. Dead to include maimed, paralyzed, comatose, castrated, disfigured, impaired by PTSD, or any other condition that will have you thinking, on a bad day, "good day to be dead."

If it's PTSD you end up with after your motorcycle crash, the cool thing is: you may get a free service dog. Won't be a top dog, like my best pal Pearl, but probably a good listener like my cat, Bunny. My brain-dead ex-dream girlfriend: Helmetless Mary, didn't even get a goldfish. Experts say some comatose people can sense their surroundings. When I'm capable, I'm going to pop over and leave Mary a fish.

Of course, it's horseshit, but I'm curious—did even

a speck of ravenously drop-dead glorious survive?

Recent safety school graduates benefit from studying a comprehensive formal curriculum compiled by
experts. Still, many prefer watching *how-to pop a
wheelie* on their phones. "No longer NimRods," they
congratulate their buddies. "Let's rip."

News reports suggest some didn't get the message.
They graduate and do something monumentally STU-
PID in less than no time, sometimes into a monument.
Blockheads! They have no respect for Rule #2. What
was Jock Crotchrocket Jones-DeSilva, today's casualty
on the local news broadcast, doing during the *How Not
to Kill Yourself* lesson? Doodling sportbike sketches
and FaceTiming his parents, whose latest news was
the emission-free tank in the garage purchased with
a government grant. *Really wanted a hydrogen fuel cell
HMMWV, but they were all out.*

With one more body added to the "splattered over
public infrastructure" statistic, Crotchrocket may well
have wished he'd removed the Brussels sprouts from
his ears and paid more attention in class. However,
we'll never know; God rest his soul because he did
something STUPID.

Thankfully, he was the only one rocketed into the
asphalt and out of his short-lived Born to be Wild life,
so all's well... that ends with only the one to blame in
the morgue. But alarmingly, the driver often is not the

only one injured. And that's downright annoying (unless they happen to be in risk management, in which case it's poetic justice).

"Perhaps you should roll Rule #2, common sense, in with Rule #1," Marta suggested. *There's no need for such esoteric nuances. We're talking throaty motorcycles, not splitting hairs.*

"Remember Marta, when Guzzi clipped the medium? Wobbled like mad, and you were scared spitless?"

Marta grinned.

"Stupid, right?"

"Taught me a lesson."

"I'll tell you what I'll do: I'll remove #2 when there are no news stories of preventable motorcycle accidents for one week." I was going to say "in the world," but I'm confident enough of its merits to limit it not just to one country, state, or province. I'll just use one city—I say "city," I mean Pirsigville, population 326. Last week it was 327—I heard there was a rider-at-fault crash out on Highway 27 on the weekend. Or, I'll remove the rule when Hell gets a light dusting of frost, or when Risk takes over the world (hmmm, sounds like a great idea for a video game.) and restricts interactions with motorcycles to our garages. Whichever comes first.

Be aware: don't turn yourself into a motorcycle statistic—even you are capable of STUPID. That's two rules. You'll be expected to know ten by the end of the book (don't cheat and look at the list in Appendix A). There's no test—that's out on the road, getting killed or not. MRR isn't like forcing a Newtonian to learn medieval Albanian poetry, Ability and Awareness have practical value. It's up to you; I'm not going to get killed because you didn't think when you took your eyes off the road and ran into a highway divider. I'll be watching for you, driving my mobility scooter, so please be careful and don't slam into me. Please tell me you remember both rules. Great; let's move on and learn Rule #3. It's very dry, but essential to not killing yourself on a motorcycle. Sorry, there's no cutting corners. Remember the last time you did that? Came close to being splattered on a long-haul semi with a skull and crossbones decal on its hood. STUPID!

RULE #3, PHYSICS

Steven Hawking wrote the acclaimed academic book, *A Brief History of Time.* It's astrophysics, or "Physics sprinkled with pixie dust," as Marta, a volunteer at MRR Labs (aka my garage), calls it. Tony, the proprietor of a local deli, has read the store's copy of Steve's book. He told me it's "flakier than my pastries," but then Tony's more of a mayonnaise guy than an astrophysics expert. Tony likes to polka and rides a scantily dressed Indian (apologies to First Nations people). Sometimes Tony and Marta ride together, Marta on her old Guzzi.

"If you're operating a deli on Earth, a thorough knowledge of condiments is of much greater value than black hole expertise," Marta reminds Tony. "I like the fact that your deli, unlike the cosmos, offers battered pickles." The sad truth is, if Tony wrote, *A Brief History of Delis*, the book would not be lauded by academia. Ditto for saving lives by sharing motorcycle ramblings. Academia is only interested in pixie dust. It's a sore point amongst deli owners and motorcycle authors.

Motorcycle physics deals with terrestrial forces, following the foundational work of Sir Isaac Newton. Pure science with no horseshit. The Laws of Motion.

The Law of Inertia. Before we carry on, please read Sir Isaac's book, *Mathematical Principles of Natural Philosophy*.

Kidding!

Sir Isaac nailed physics, never rode, but is the grandfather of modern motorcycle engineering. Newtonian physics is nothing like the ancient Greek musings presented in the *Zen* book. Valentino Rossi didn't study abstract ideas or political science to learn how to get around corners safely, and neither should you. You're a motorcyclist, not ET, Uranus (the ancient Greek God), René Descartes, or Karl Marx.

Before we start, please ensure you have a calculator app, a picture of IBM's Watson computer, Mr. Newton's portrait, or a slide rule (for very old schoolers) in view. You won't be required to use them, but occasionally lift your gaze from the text to take a visual reminder of the topic. It's what educators call a "training aid." The image will remain with you and help you remember Rule #3, the way a sexy pinup arouses, like Mary in her glorious bikini days, if you want to contemplate things other than physics.

In honor of Sir Isaac, MRR Labs presents the following rule:

Rule #3: Ignoring Motorcycle Physics May Kill You

Marta made up a corollary: studying astrophysics will not help you on-motorcycle, unless confronted by a pothole the size of a black hole.

My mastery of the Newtonian Laws Concerning Motorcycles was initially limited to what is achievable riding a small displacement dirt bike in the desert (although my yellow Suzuki TS-125 was relatively large and conspicuous in a city teeming with mopeds). If only Newton had lined up his apples in the sand, at regular intervals, to teach me how to brake, lean, and counter-steer. Occasionally throwing dates and goat horns to test my reflexes. That man knew his stuff, apples, and lean angles. Perhaps when bikes travel on Mars, Steve's book will find a spot on the shelves of motorcycle engineers.

◆ ◆ ◆

I had to wait until I returned home to the west coast to really absorb Rule #3. You don't do a great deal of high-speed highway driving on a TS-125, and the physics of navigating a small dirt bike up a hard pack sand hill, is pretty much instinctual when you're young. Even Moses figured it out, and, like me, he never attended Parking Lot Cone School.

In the desert, there are no corners that tighten up in a decreasing radius. Drifting wide in a wide-open space is not a big deal. It won't end your life. You have two hundred miles or so of space to get your machine under control. Lean into the wind. Let the bike fly. There is no need to haul out the Laws of Motion or study the formulas you slept through in high school to correct your behaviour. Just drift. Enjoy a battered pickle or two.

Fortunately, by the time I discovered tight curves on man-made highways, YouTube had the science of motorcycle physics down. Video experts explained what not to do when the choices, depending on your direction of travel, seem to be: run wide and rocket off a cliff or collide head-on into Mach truck—hone your motorcycle physics-based skills like countersteering, they suggested. Navigating corners on a bike is much more complex than calculating the mass of an atomic atom which, as we know, every time we do the math is the same (1.67×10-27 kilograms, for one of the periodic elements, is it carbon or that new one, ununseptium)? Doesn't matter; ask Marta if it's troubling you. Math isn't nebulous, which is why Watson is so good at it. But put Watson on a KTM, and he's lost.

Atomic mass is predictable. Corners, though? Same answer each time? Not a chance. The question doesn't even stay the same. A corner on a motorcycle is a crap shoot; weather, road conditions, traffic, wildlife, radius, slope, and your skill level are all at play. Especially your skill level, so thank the stars you respect Rule #3. And that's only ONE corner–there's another one just down the ribbon of black twisting asphalt, and then a thousand more—a thousand potentially lethal questions. The physics is constantly in motion, testing the rider's skills. You don't have to geek out on Newton's formulas and logic. Understanding how to apply his body of knowledge is what Rule #3 is all about, mainly how to lean, counter-steer, brake, and throttle control. Read *A Brief History of Time* but keep your rubber on Earth.

Interestingly, unlike nuclear physics or painting, riding requires both left and right sides of the brain to function in tandem. Michelangelo's left brain slept through much of his gorgeous work on the Sistine Chapel. Robert Oppenheimer didn't use his right brain when he invented the atomic bomb. Perhaps he should have? Try using a single side of your brain when you're motorcycle riding, and You Will Die. Monday mornings tend to see neither side of my brain functioning, let alone in tandem. They may start waking up by lunchtime. Left will go back to sleep by midnight. Brain Brian usually stays up a while longer. Be Brain Aware before you climb on and twist the throttle. Are both sides on duty? Know that while Sir Isaac could depict motion using formulae, he could not ride. Leonardo da Vinci had perfect left-right balance and would have cleaned up at MottoE race events.

Be skillful: study motorcycle physics. But remember, not all coconuts are designed to be placed inside a helmet. Practice tuning up your tandem brain with exercises like: counteract target fixation: look where you want to go.

Away from the desert, on a good old fashion twisty two-lane western highway, before I'd fully absorbed Rule #3, I realized: I'm going to kill myself trying to keep pace with my race-track-friendly riding buddies. They understand high speed, braking, and cornering physics. I spent my time trying to avoid death under entirely different circumstances. Fly by the Seat of Your Pants School had gaps that could turn deadly. Inadvertently I may do something STUPID. I didn't confess, "Hey guys, I don't have a clue about high-speed cornering. My school didn't have cones or corners. Please teach me your ways," because, like most illiterate adults, my lack of formal education embarrassed me. Instead, I boned up... for safer bones. I learned on the sly. It's not complicated if you have YouTube. Unlike riding in the desert, knowing the science of riding fast and surviving is crucial for highway riders. As is the art of slow-speed maneuvering, on bikes larger than a TS-125. Ever had an 800lb / 365kg Goldwing topple over on you?

With more appreciation for the principles of inertia and momentum, I was soon scraping pegs on corners without the terrifying fear of death lurking over me, and I stopped panic-braking–a telltale sign of a Blockhead with little knowledge of Rule #3. I understood the importance of preserving space. One day I may become Leonardo DaVinci-like and qualify for the Isle of Man TT, but for now, I'll settle for not freaking out and doing the wrong thing at the wrong time. I prefer not to kill myself when I'm out on a rip, twisting the throttle, saying hello Life, the Beautiful, don't be stupid, master Rule #3.

It was different in the early days of motorcycling. Physics wasn't all about mastering speed. A 1968 BSA Rocket 3, or a similar age bike, and a Hayabusa or Livewire, are different machines. BSA riders didn't have to master rocket-like acceleration and ridiculously high speeds. They could get away with Rule #3, Lite. Technical riding skills used to be the dominion of track professionals; today, everyone's a Valentino Rossi. So please don't wait till you're drifting wide into oncoming traffic to say to yourself, guess I shouldn't have ignored motorcycle physics. *This YZF-R1 sure's a lot peppier than dad's old R50.*

Today, thanks to clever engineering, riding skills can be tucked away in abeyance much of the time. Riders can concentrate on traffic and road conditions while their machines guide themselves through curves, correct panic-braking, and other bad habits motorcycle engineers have compensated for. Modern motorcycles can bore because they often demand little of the driver. But it's like using a spellchecker. You no longer need to spell, right? WRONG! Only if you want to come across as an illiterate Blockhead. You must have language skills tucked away, ready to deploy when spellchecker trips over a "to" that should have been "too" and kicks off WWIII.

Engineers have transferred responsibilities from drivers to sensors and computer brains, making riders complacent. But there's always a pop quiz up ahead. Our driver is on auto-drive, traveling far faster than an old-school track racer. The sun blinds at the apex of a tight curve. If your technical riding skills aren't honed and ready to deploy instantaneously, Deadeye will have you in his sights. Finito! *Physic skills could have gotten you out of that nasty drift, but you relied on natural ability. Oh well, another notch for the Dickster.*

Instead of tinkering with pipe audio dynamics, devote time to learning about front-end rake, trail geometry, and camber thrust.

Speed reduces time. I'm not going to drone on about how that complicates Rule #3. Check out Steve's *Time* book. Tony, at the deli, will lend you the store copy if you purchase the *Cosmic Special*. It comes with two battered pickles.

Motorcycle education is not a physics class or an elegant art lesson. It's more like painting with calculus. If you don't want to do the math, stay the hell off the highway! If you don't like art... you got it: also stay the hell off the highway. Make sure both sides of your brain are in the game. For me, that's the aforementioned noon to midnight window. I'm titling too far toward Sir Isaac or Pablo Picasso outside of that time frame. I must stay *off-motorcycle*.

Isn't it enough that everyone, including yourself,

is out to kill you? Must you also ignore the laws of physics? Take Dicky D. Despite his natural marksmanship, did he rest on his laurels like his brother Radical? No, he devoured the mental and technical knowledge necessary to win a boat load of marksmanship gold ribbons and wreak havoc at the carnival. Motorcycles and guns are both dangerous. If you can't be bothered to educate yourself, take Risk Mitigation Guy's advice and hunker down, sitting in a tank, going nowhere. Or, like our carnival ducks, you can only hope that your dumb luck doesn't run out.

Leonardo da Vinci Vs. Valentino Rossi. Who wins? Let Marta know.

RULE #4, KILLER BIKES

Have you seen the movie Christine? About a Plymouth Fury with paranormal super-powers and an evil mind of its own? Christine is a car that goes on vendettas and kills people. For research purposes, Marta arranged a viewing in my garage, or as we call it, the Lab, along with The Car and Maximum Overdrive. Unsalted, butterless popcorn, plus tap water provided—lots of grumbling about the cuisine. "Next time, Brussels sprouts," Marta announced! Did I mention the Lab staff are all volunteers? A few retirees and a couple of out-of-work types, hoping "MRR Labs" will look good on their resumes. They're not "in it for the money," but I haven't yet figured out what they are in it for. Still, I must encourage Marta to loosen up on the snack budget.

One retiree has white coat syndrome. Likes to dress up in the recycled lab uniforms Marta wrangled as a donation. Unlike the other volunteers, he has no interest in motorcycles. "I'm a trout fisher," he declares proudly as if it's a superior calling. How do you fire an annoying, scatterbrained trout fishing volunteer? I think I'll assign that task to Marta. She's been chomping at the bit.

Here's the logic the folks in my garage grappled with as they dislodged bits of popcorn from between their teeth:

If Buddha can live in motorcycle circuitry, as suggested in the Zen book and applauded by epistemologists, can the Devil also take up residence in electronic components?

To quote Lab findings, "The notion that the devil can be embedded in a bike is **balderdash.** The devil-car theory lacks credibility and is a lackluster attempt at the quick buck school of marketing. With the motorcycle JOY shield up and Buddha on board, the Devil hasn't a chance. The Killer Bike phenomenon originates with human error—primarily inappropriate selection and neglect," or as Marta puts it, "dumbasses not paying attention to Rule #2."

Other than trout fisher, the lab volunteers are all pretty clever. Clever enough not to find jobs, just ride, I suppose.

My first motorcycle was the exact opposite of a Killer Bike. I bought it five years after the publication of *Zen and the Art of Motorcycle Maintenance.* Young, curious, and restless, I was more interested in Zen and the Art of Farting Around than motorcycles. I'd putted around on friends' small bikes, mostly on dirt roads. Had someone predicted, "One day you will own a motorcycle as your sole source of transportation," I'd have answered "nonsense. I'm pragmatic. A technologist. Ones and zeros. Newtonian physics. Why drive an impractical toy when I can buy a car? Where would I put my stuff? Or Mary, if she agrees to go out with me? Besides, the weather can suck and I might die." I wasn't familiar with Killer Bikes at the time; there are lots of less dangerous reasons not to own a motorcycle. I agreed with all of them.

Here's how destiny got flipped around, and I became the proud owner of a cheerful Suzuki.

At age twenty-six, I sold everything I'd accumulated in life to that point, which could be defined as "a bunch of mostly worthless crap," to work for an engineering company on the other side of the globe. I'm somewhat older now, yet I seem to have bought pretty much all the crap back again. I'm a technologist, not an engineer which isn't great if you're working for a consulting engineering company. Like Junior Nurse in an office of uppity specialists. "Bed pan call on the design floor. Calling, Mr. Stewart!" Thank god Larry's funding came through to help make MRR Labs a reality. He left me $1,464 in his will following the death-by-seaweed cracker incident "for your dangerous motorcycle hobby." I budgeted $732 for snacks, under Marta's control, and spent $23.16 on a Larry Memorial Plaque. Marta added "Budget Management" to her resume, "In case I allow myself to be hired."

Living in an apartment in large, hot, polluted, chaotic Middle East City, I made friends with another expatriate and his wife. They had dual-purpose 250cc motorcycles shipped from Vancouver, Canada (engine size was capped at 250). The couple rode their bikes

on hard-pack desert sand and used their Citroën 2CV,
the weird French two-cylinder, air-cooled, economy
car for urban driving. They were wise and chose not
to ride in undisciplined city traffic, understood Motorcycle Riding Rule #1, owned a car, and acted accord-
ingly. "There is MAGIC in the machines and JOY on-
motorcycle," they told me.

I thought they might be weirdos—many ex-pats
live outside the norm. I was aware of the wonders
of sex, travel, and food but had never witnessed the
eye-sparkle of people recalling the Joy of Motorcycles.
"Ride in any direction. Discover ancient ruins… old
caravanserai. Eat in central courtyards where weary
travelers rested hundreds of years earlier. Visit remote
villages and meet the shy, hospitable people those an-
cestors have lived in the area for centuries."

So, I said, "Teach me your ways." My first biker
commitment.

Politics, religion, colonialism, totalitarianism, and
other socio-economic-isms ran rampant in that part
of the world. But I won't go there. *Scraping Pegs* has its
plateful, bringing the truth about motorcycles down
to earth. Societal issues? That's another kettle of fish
best left for a different chef. Or is it? Motorcycles can
produce moments of Absolute Clarity for riders with a
Motorcycle State of Mind. Perfectly balanced thought,
stripped of baggage. Do riders not have an obligation
to share their profound, uncaged visionary solutions
for the betterment of humanity? Political science is
struggling; some suggest it's on the verge of calling in
the armed forces. Unlike on-motorcycle or engineer-

ing labs, the UN Secretariat Building produces tittle-tattle, not rational thought. Surely, the phony-baloney scientists, dictators, and politicians would welcome a helping hand?

The year before I crashed, I rode the Pacific Coast Highway. There was a tremendous amount of political theatre in the water, air, and lying on the asphalt. It was inescapable, and so thick it threatened to push me into uneasiness. I rode until this moment of Absolute Clarity eased my mind and scraped my pegs:

Constitutions worldwide must mandate leaders walk or ride motorcycles (where ever possible). Will you be taking Motorcycle One today, President Rider? Our leaders would get along famously if we took their armored limos away and plunked them down on two-wheelers. Get them out of the cages that wall them off from the people they adore and strive to serve. Isn't that what they're always going on and on about?

Place them closer to the citizenry, the group they sacrifice their wealth and freedom to serve. Instead of hiding behind endless reports, have them ride through the environment they cherish and promise to protect. Life embraces motorcycle riders. Cruising around their dominions would connect our rulers, not wall them off, isolated in the back of chauffeur-driven cages, denigrating people sitting in the back of other luxury polluters. Sure Deadeye, or this brother, Radical Dick would pick off a few, but fresh blood is golden in the leadership game. There is never a shortage of egomaniacs prepared to step up and serve the citizenry.

Motorcycles are excellent Thinking Machines. Which profession is most in need of help with THINKING?

> *Truth About Motorcycles: the world would be a better place if the people-in-charge were touched by Motorcycle JOY.*

Motorcycles lead riders to inspired answers. They screen out folks whose left and right brains don't work well in tandem; people incapable of operating motorcycles sure as hell shouldn't be running countries! "Or hamlets, either," Marta pointed out when I filled her in on my proposal.

Isn't that all we want from our leaders—intelligent answers, getting along, and well-balanced brain functionality? No flipping out about left and right politics. Sure, a few outliers would sneak in, like North Korea playing the extreme hermit chopper dude, but generally, motorcycling is a welcoming community. So, let's sell the UN building, fire the chauffeurs, donate the limos to one of those boots-on-the-ground charities run by volunteers (like MRR Labs), buy each leader a bike and a helmet, and tell them not to come back until they have solid pragmatic solutions and are all pals. Ride an electric bike if you're anti-fossil fuel. No excuses. No tribalism! No more theater games! Fact-based reporters may tag along. #WorldLeadersOnBikes. We'll clue them in on the Motorcycle Riding Rules, and teach them to change their oil, before The-World-is-My-Oyster-and-We're-Going-to-Save-It, road trip takes the starter's flag.

Don't you think world leaders should know how to change their oil? Shouldn't that come before changing the socioeconomics of a country? If you can balance a motorcycle, there's a chance you may balance your country's budget. If you stop to assist stranded riders, you'll likely give our forsaken a hand up.

What's the downside? "Riders couldn't possibly screw things up worse than political science," Marta said.

"The answer always is, ride."

"World, rejoice."

I didn't have moments of Absolute Clarity before motorcycle; I was plodding through life, like everyone else who doesn't ride, in a brain fog, buying junk I didn't need—living in a room on the outskirts of Blobland. I didn't have a plan to ride a motorcycle on secondary roads to Yellowstone, postulating along the way (like in the *Zen* book).

A Suzuki TS-125 (with a dual gear shift, giving it eight gears and lots of range) started me on my Road to Joy. I had zero motorcycle smarts (Marta says I'm lacking in several other departments as well, like budget allocation and firing dumbasses. I didn't comparison shop because almost everyone in the country rode mopeds or donkeys. It was just dumb luck. I ended up with one of the best starter bikes possible. And it had pizazz; compared with the hordes of scooters and mules in the city, I rode a large machine that rose above the crowd. From zero to proud motorcycle owner, just like that. I loved that little yellow bike from the first rev of its engine. Well, maybe from day two because, truth be told, my friend drove it home from the shop while I sat on the back. "Hung on for dear life" might be a better description, second-guessing my madness at every intersection. Even then, I thought *everyone wants to kill us.*

In short, TS-125 was a peace-loving, happy, well-adjusted machine. Undoubtedly a genetic mutation, being a direct descendent of the first dirt bike. TS-125 would be personable in any environment. I assumed all bikes were like that, well-adjusted, happy wanderers.

I would learn the hard way that not all bikes are your friend. Poor selection, or neglect, can wake an inanimate machine and turn it against you.

Rule #4: Your Motorcycle May Be Trying To Kill You.

I bought a Honda CR500cc two-stroke, single-cylinder, dual-purpose bike after politics forced me to leave the desert and abandon TS-125. I still worry about my baby, like if you had no choice but to abandon a loving pet, you never stop wondering, *what became of my best friend?*

Thumper and I never bonded.

I used simple math to pick out Thumper: naturally, with an engine four times larger, it would be four hundred percent better. Wrong! Too much Left-brain while ignoring Brain Brian. Try four hundred percent worse! It had a hair-trigger and low-end torque comparable to a well-tuned North Korean missile.

Like an unreliable slingshot, Thumper attempted to rocket me to my death on several occasions. No longer riding in wide-open spaces, cliffs, trees, boulders, and other nat-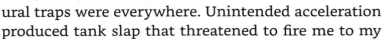
ural traps were everywhere. Unintended acceleration produced tank slap that threatened to fire me to my

drooling days. Had Thumper been my first bike, it may well have succeeded in its murderous attempts. Thankfully, TS-125 had imparted just enough throttle control and other physics smarts to save my bacon.

TS-125's teachings failed to protect me from another murderous motorcycle, Movie Bike, a sassy BMW 1200C cruiser built for James Bond's use in the movie, *Tomorrow Never Dies*. I'm not guilty of Motorcycle Neglect; like Thumper, Movie Bike was a Selection Error. Looking back, it was an obvious, ill-considered, impulsive choice. I was infatuated with its appearance and ignored physics—way too much Brain Brian. Hollywood hadn't called.

"Did you think you were Pierce Bronson," Marta asked?

"People say I remind them of Keanu Reeves."

I knew Marta was thinking: horseshit!

I was touring with packs of bikes engineered for covering ground, not posing on movie sets. My clear-headed friends rode big road-hugging adventure bikes and other serious machines that glue themselves to surfaces, ready to go anywhere and tackle anything. They built my bike to look good. It constantly whined: "please, can we stop now? I want to pose. Look, people! Park me, park me! I'm a preening movie star: you'd love to ride me." Movie Bike liked to get its own way, do its thing. A rider admiring my BMW cruiser, told me, "It's like a beautiful woman. Great to look at, but not very practical." Here's a popular expression you should apply when selecting your motorcycle (or trout fishing rod):

Beauty is more than skin deep. Ask yourself, how is this bike's (rod's) physics?

Movie Bike

I gathered in a gang of six one weekend, our bikes headed to central Oregon. They, with their rugged machines in a muscled platoon, me driving the equivalent of a lightly armored vehicle forced to stay out of the action, toting toilet paper and gun lube for the warriors upfront. Stay behind where it's safe! Despite my riding choice, I tried to go where the pack went. Did what the brigade did. It embarrassed me to admit I'd selected a machine incapable of keeping up. "I'll see you there in a few days. Movie Bike has a curtain call and autograph scheduling conflict."

We rode off the Washington State Ferry in Anacortes, prepared for rain. The sky obliged and soon opened up in a torrential downpour, unusual for the wet drizzly Pacific Northwest. Determined to traverse the mountain pass to reach our motel for the night in the dry interior, the gang pressed on.

In terrible visibility, we entered a Burlington roundabout. That's when the mishap occurred. I was distracted (yes, that's a rule for later) by the rain, the traffic, the visibility. Movie Bike, ever the self-deterministic type, clearly wanted to pull over, probably to cower under a tree and snap a pic for Instagram. My mates' bikes quickly changed lanes to reach the highway exit. Their bikes didn't want to kill them; not true of old Movie Bike.

Movie Bike tripped over its tires as it changed lanes, catching the slippery white dividing line and slipping out from under me in a shower of spray and sparks, scraping pegs in a bad way. It tried to slide elegantly, aware of the ever-present mobile phone with instantaneous upload to Tiktok and Instagram. I lay spread-eagled in the middle of the roundabout, stunned and winded, waiting for the afternoon traffic to crush me. But Movie Bike didn't care. Passing motorists gawked from their windows at the celebrity bike, "Bond's the name, James Bond," and pointed at the world's greatest spy sprawled in the middle of a roundabout in Burlington, Washington. "Shouldn't he be in London meeting with MI5? Saving the world from evil overlords?"

Luckily, they didn't run me over. "007 dead!" would have screamed the global headlines causing the Queen to shed a tear and cuddle with her corgis (dogs have natural Mutt JOY and are a good option in the absence of a motorcycle).

I should have been overjoyed, lying uninjured on the wet asphalt, but I was rattled and pissed off! "Stupid Movie Bike," I told the guys on their powerful machines, stating the obvious, that the fall had nothing to do with my skill level. So, I kicked the stricken bike to emphasize the point. It didn't hurt because I had my Lunar Rover Moonboots on. On a GS, I, too, would have kept the rubber side down. My friends rallied around–it's good to be with riders capable of sorting things out. The pack gave the fallen BMW the evil eye, "you're a silly bike. You Harley wannabe."

The rain eased during the MacGyvering. You know, MacGyver—the guy from the TV series who could fix anything with duct tape and a paper clip? Scratch that... He'd *build* a vehicle with duct tape and a paper clip. When the bike was drivable, I let myself be persuaded not to turn back. Though bruised and recovering from embarrassment, Movie Bike and I followed the herd, sandwiched between a GS front and rear guard for protection. *Forward the Light Brigade! Charge for the hills.*

I sold Movie Bike just as soon as we returned home. It never completed its deadly mission but did wound my Motorcycle Pride.

The point is that motorcycles come in many styles, each with its own flavors. Of course, not all models will be a match, like TS-125. I'm not James Bond; Movie Bike and I were not a suitable pair. So, asking a Movie Bike to run with adventure bikes turned it into a Killer Bike. Thumper was too big and way too torquey for the riding I was doing. I was guilty of making Selection Errors, resulting in bikes with murderous intentions.

In my defence, no one explained that I should be on the outlook for Doctor Doom hitching a ride. I thought all bikes were cheerful, sweet, and well adjusted, with Buddha riding along in the electrics.

Do your homework. Buy an appropriate bike for your skill level, size, and strength. For example, a big heavy machine, requiring a lot of force to make it lean into a corner, may kill you. Too powerful (like Thumper), and the bike may take control from you. There are lots of well-engineered choices: Royal Enfield, Harley Davidson, Kawasaki, Triumph, KTM, Pliaggio and more. Keep your machine in good working order, and it will remain faithful. A good-natured dog in the wrong hands can turn into a killer—not the canine's fault! Be aware; it's the same with motorcycles. Neglect your bike, and it will go from puppy dog to monster, from well-behaved to mauling its owner. Bald tires and dodgy brakes are just waiting for Rule #4 and Doctor Doom to kick your ass.

Dumping your Killer Bike need not be an ethical dilemma. There is no need to fret about being scolded on Judgement Day if you are a responsible seller. "You're the one who sold that Killer Bike to Mary McGregor, right?"

"Yes."

"Of course, I'm right. Did they not teach you about rhetorical questions on Earth? Or Motorcycle Responsibility?"

In this situation, heaven applicants can only grin like nutters.

"You didn't think to, at least, throw in your old, dirty, spare helmet to protect Mary's gorgeous head? And force her to put it on before she wheelied out of your driveway? Have you not heard of accountability?"

The right buyer will tame your Killer Bike, causing it to lose its murderous inclinations. Give Doctor Doom the heave-ho. Even make it cheerful. For instance, Movie Bike would be perfect for local TV weather personality Eddie Edwards. Eddie likes to pose and cruise slowly where he can be seen. Stop and take selfies with fans. Just don't ask, "Any better weather headed our way, Eddie?" He hates that. It could cause him to do something STUPID.

Brussels sprouts are the equivalent of eating slimy, raw slugs for everyone but a few Flemish outliers. A Flemish-like connoisseur can take you off the hook. You must find Killer's soul mate. The equivalent of Mr. De Smet, Brussels sprout enthusiast. "Enjoying your raw slugs, Mr. De Smet?" Like there are sprout lovers, someone is a match for your Selection Error. On Judgement Day, God will congratulate you. "Good job sorting out that Killer Bike situation, Roy. Were you aware the Devil was trying to weasel into its circuitry? Gave up when you sold it to Mr. De Smet. It was exactly what he needed—a much better job than the Blockhead who sold his bike to Mary MacGregor. Go on to Heaven. I'll have the other guy do a stint in Motorcycle Seat Hell.

*Humans hate to admit mistakes: Don't nurse a
cantankerous bike; dump it before it dumps you.*

TS-125 was as far removed from being a killer
as it's possible to get. I wonder what became of my
capable friend? Hope she didn't have to lug shackled
lambs to their death.

I'm wandering, losing my train of thought in a
warren of side streets. Time to slap myself and focus.
Are you ready for another rule?

RULE #5, COMPLACENT

I struggled with Motorcycle Riding Rule #5. It's hard to be constantly on the lookout when nothing happens. It's like working as a security guard at a Brussels sprout factory when the harvest of decent food was abundant. What's the point? Does anyone give a worn sprocket? A tree could do my job. I'll play on my phone rather than scan for nonexistent threats. One day Radical Dick sneaks up, crawling on his belly in the dirt, rifle strapped to his back, hunting knife between his teeth. He sights the Wordle playing sentry in and squeezes the trigger. Wounds him with his third bullet (Radical isn't a marksman like his little brother, but is a better orator) and then slits the sentry's throat. Hello, Flemish-Luxembourger-Prussian Major Veggie Conflict! You never can tell when a guard will lose concentration or a motorcyclist will slip into Blobland and be torpedoed into Complacency Swamp.

Rule #5: Complacency Can Kill You!

Truth About Motorcycles: riding
can be monotonous.

As Marta says: "Sometimes it sucks, and sometimes it doesn't." It's not a surprise. Eating, sex, watching TV; overdo anything, and it becomes bland, humans get bored. Spice sex up by wearing a tutu, or by playing Russian Roulette while watching sports, or twisting the throttle. Boredom produces complacency, leading to sluggish reactions and doing something stupid. Complacency on a bike can kill you. Parking Lot Cone School teaches technique but developing and maintaining a Motorcycle State of Mind requires constant THINKING to remain Alert.

Rule #5 was never an issue driving TS-125 around Middle Eastern City. Noise, chaos, animal slaughter, and human misery kept me constantly alert. No hidden snipers. The odd hidden snake. Cager-killers drove out in the open. For citizens, murder by vehicle was a misdemeanor. At times chaos scared the kebabs out of me. Rule #5 loves that. It keeps you on your toes. It loathes dull, constantly signaling, "Mr. Dick, over there. Sitting duck in a massive complacency fog! Easy shot! Even Radical could nail this bored duck."

Prairie grasslands are beautiful, but their highways are never-ending straight stretches of nothingness. You hope a damsel in distress will dart out from behind one of those trees planted as feeble protection against the wind, but she won't. The flatlands challenge Itchy Boots, and even Rule #5 falls asleep. Bikes seek corners; they deplore straight. You do too. It causes you to switch cruise control on or flip-down your throttle lock. Fire up your playlist. Fiddle with the Bluetooth controls on your helmet. Two hours of drudgery since you left the Nothingness Coffee Shop and Truck Stop. *Wasn't this supposed to be outlaw exciting?* But you're marooned in Complacency Wheatland. A little worried about bored cops, but where would they hide? Suddenly your bike dives into a huge pothole. Or was it a black hole? You were busy playing with the controls on your GPS instead of scanning the highway, watching for Mr. Dick. Over the bars, you go to join sweet Mary McGregor. Neck snaps. Luckily for you, just paralyzed from the neck down, not brain dead thanks to your new certified helmet. *Rule #5! Rule #5! Rule #5!* Repeat as often as necessary. It can save your life. It's not a complicated rule, BE AWARE. Complacency kills!

Truth About Motorcycles: constantly remaining on your toes isn't easy.

Complacency can also nail you off-motorcycle. Maintenance slips. The tires that should have been replaced aren't. *Fuck this, good enough.* "I'll get to it next year," you shrug off an overdue repair job. The precheck is always the same so skip it. Then, one day along comes Dr. Doom. *How about this bike? Its vacancy sign is on.* Step right up and slide into the thingamabob, Dr. Doom.

The tedium fix is throttle up. Pump adrenaline

through veins and into the brain. Fire up your neuro-transmitters. Complacency is replaced by Rule #2, doing something stupid. See how the Motorcycle Riding Rules interconnect? Marta's working on a flow-chart to illustrate the interaction. It's a big job. I hope she doesn't say, "Fuck it! Good enough," before she's finished. I'll hang her chart on the garage wall next to *Motorcycle on Velvet*.

I mustn't become complacent about what happened to Bob? "Bunny, want to jump up? On my lap. Let's do some thinking, shall we? Is it possible Bob became complacent?"

RULE #6, CHOICES

My cat's called Bunny because he killed the next-door neighbor's rabbit.

Kidding!

Bunny likes to sleep in the rabbit hutch with Hammy, a real rabbit who thinks he's a pig. When I see them together, I wonder, is Hammy getting too complacent?

We often sit together in the lab-garage. Bunny sticks his claws in my pant leg and pulls himself up to relax on my lap. Sometimes his claws dig into my skin, and I set Pearl, my dog, on him. Don't worry. Pearl's a licker.

Bunny's some kind of exotic Siamese, a cat person told me. I don't know. When I picked him up for free, he was "looking for a good home." We were "looking for a good cat" to replace our dead one, Squirrely. I paid more attention to the "free" part than the "exotic" part.

I run theories about what happened to Bob by Bunny. He's very receptive and respectful, unlike my wife, who shoots me her, *enough about* Bob, glare. Bunny purrs and massages until he eventually falls asleep. Do cats sleep? Bunny appears to nod off, but I suspect some part of his brain is constantly on guard.

Probably for Pearl, who sulks whenever Bunny and I enjoy quality time. Hammy couldn't care less—rabbits just like to eat and make baby rabbits. They're not good contemplators like Bunny. Especially rabbits that think they're pigs.

Bunny is what neurologists call a "memory trigger," and I have what doctors call "a brain that needs triggering." I made a few triggers up to placate my doc. Here's how I explained my Bunny trigger to Dr. Li, who thinks it's a good idea to do brain exercises:

1. When I see Bunny;
2. *The phrase, "There is more than one way to skin a cat," pops into my frontal lobe;*
3. Often accompanied by horrific images of bunnies being skinned alive;
4. My brain interprets the saying as *there are multiple ways to achieve a goal*;
5. And remembers Rule #6! Rule #6! It's all about making smart choices!
6. Thanks, Bunny!

If your brain is sieve-like, consider developing a few Motorcycle Riding Rule memory triggers to exercise your noggin. It won't seem so silly if you make a game out of it. After all:

Rule #6: Your Noggin Can Save You.

This rule is the flip side of Rule #2, where Stupid You was trying to kill you. Here Clever You is trying to keep you out of harm's way. Rather more preferable, right? When your riding buddy goes on a rip in terrible conditions, and you're not at your best, use your noggin. Don't chase.

Don't follow that bike weaving dangerously through traffic. Weaving is always dangerous; use your noggin and choose a safer option like knitting (careful of the long needles). Lane splitting where there's no margin–could marginally split you instead. Your buddy nails a tricky jump and eggs you to do it too–well, eggs splatter, so make a smart choice. Pressured to buy a motorcycle beyond your skill level, but just like your buddies–ask your pals if they'd like the pressure of that motorcycle lying on top of them in a ditch. Thought not.

Part of using Rule #6 is not allowing others to put you in a position where riding may kill you. Instead, reject dangerous peer pressure and showmanship. You're no army recruit following Loo-ten-ant Foolish Dan on a suicide mission. On this occasion, what your mother told you was right: "Just because Amber drives her bike like an out-of-control meth freak, doesn't mean you have to! If she rode her bike off a cliff, would you follow?" Maybe back in the day. But now you don't use meth; you use your noggin!

Rule #1 embed the fact that you're in a war and everyone is trying to kill you. Beyond the killing fields, there is JOY, so you ride on. Think of #6 as the commander of your *Zone of Awareness*. Looks like DD is behind the wheel of the black pickup truck (#1). Better watch the front wheels (#6).

Marta calls #6 "the no-brainer rule" because "it's so obvious." But it's not that simple. Think of it this way: did you ace the big calculus exam back in junior high? Unless your name is Sir Isaac Newton, probably not. Every question on that exam had a factual answer —answers within the grasp of most human brains. If you had used your noggin effectively, you wouldn't have bombed. Today you'd be an astrophysicist instead of battering pickles for Tony at his deli. Noggins require discipline. Many don't like to do calculus. *On-motorcycle,* you must always do the math. Keep your coconut dialed-in. Maybe *coconut* would be a good memory trigger for Rule #6?

"#6 reminds me of Movie Bike," Marta stated bluntly before crunching a battered pickle. "You were guilty of not using your noggin and did something stupid. Maybe it wasn't a Killer Bike after all?"

Thanks for pointing that out, Marta. Yes, I followed, failed to act, even though I knew it was dicey. The rules interacted and Movie Bike tried to kill me. Should I blame myself for not Using My Noggin? Or for being Stupid? Here's an essential tip for handling tough questions from the Marta's of the world:

If you're involved in a preventable and embarrassing situation, like I was with Movie Bike, where the incident is traceable to multiple root causes, ALWAYS pin the blame on the Rule that doesn't make you look like a complete jackass. That's using your noggin!

"Definitely a Killer Bike, Marta. There's more evidence than just the roundabout story." Did she buy it? No, but Marta understands how sensitive I am and has learned to respect my feelings.

Bunny understands. I insisted Marta include my cat and dog in the lab snack order. She agreed with this condition: dependent on Tony increasing the lab's battered pickle discount. She wants a free pickle for every six purchased. Seems fair. Tony countered with an offer to double the loan period for the deli's copy of *A Brief History of Time*. "It's a bit of a pickle," Marta said in her update. I suspect they'll reach an agreement after riding.

Motorcyclists are a diverse bunch. Cruisers, sports bikes, scooters, trial bikes, adventure bikes, sidecars, touring bikes. There is more than one way to skin a cat, remember? Take Classic Bikers (CBers). They keep the past alive, nursing their aging iron horses with noggins that use old-school thinking. Bikes others look upon as scrap metal, CBer brains somehow turn into show pieces. Tradition is everything to this respected group of two-wheel historians—masters of machine tools. Possessors of sage-like secrets and brains exploding with knowledge. During each group ride, their bikes must be rewired, or the carburetor cleaned, but they use their noggins and somehow get it done. They're off Deadeye's radar much of the time because they're busy cleaning up oil leaks or machining valve seats. They all use their copy of *Zen and the Art of Motorcycle Maintenance*, to prop up the back tire.

Classic Bikers and Zero SR or S1000RR riders sit at opposite ends of the motorcycle spectrum. Engineers design today's machines to be wizards. There's no pulling over, unwrapping the small tool kit that waits under the seat and using your noggin to over-haul the engine. There is no wedging foil across con-tacts or cranking the oversized adjustment screw to be on your way. Riders can't fix their modern machine without a software patch and the secret tools Service keeps locked away. No wonder classic and modern bike owners come up with different answers to the same questions. Both climb on alone. They THINK in the saddle, but their brains produce different instruc-tions. One swerves right; the other brakes. One is not correct, the other wrong. There is more than one way and plenty of wrong ways *to skin a cat.* Your noggin must produce its own split-second decisions.

Motorcycles have become more complex, but eas-ier to ride, reducing brain load. There's trickery in modern machines. It's an unintended consequence of engineering excellence. Old BSA Rocket 3s came with built-in reminders to keep riders alert. Asses got pounded, fingers turned numb, and noggins yelled, "Enough! Pull this contraption over. Please, let's tinker with the carburetor for a while. Get me off this damn bucket of bolts! It's given me a BSA of a head ache!"

Modern bikes trick riders into believing their bike will do much of the driving. Don't listen. Remember Rule #6! Use Your Noggin!

Don't blindly rely on your motorcycle's capabilities; make use of the computer in your head! Rule #6! Rule #6! Your smart bike can't save you!

Are modern bikes too clever? Not if riders absorb Rule #6 and stay in the game.

It's too bad political science won't ask motorcycle

engineers for help. Quit arguing about the seating plan for the *Official World Summit* in Bali and seek assistance. If political scientists outsourced their responsibilities to motorcycle engineers, the engineers would perfect the base platforms from which societies flourish in no time. From stable bikes to stable societies, both with auto-correction features for Blockhead and Nimrod operators. It's an obvious solution, but if your unbalanced brain gets tripped up by peak, peek, and pique, like they say, "You can't see the wheel for the spokes."

This Save The World scenario came to me while riding in Tennessee. As I've said, motorcycles are terrific Thinking Machines. They fire up both sides of your brain. Produce moments of Absolute Clarity like replacing political scientists with motorcycle engineers. And risk mitigation lawyers with political scientists (why not throw them a bone)? I'm not vindictive.

If you happen to be in Tennessee, switch MRR to High, and ride the Tail of the Dragon—enjoy 318 glorious curves in 11 miles. Don't think about saving the world. Just ride. Motorcycles are for escaping.

Marta looked up the on-line definition of "political science." We had a good laugh. "Political Science is thus an organized body of knowledge the facts of which have been scientifically and systematically observed collected and classified and from these facts are formulated and proved a series of propositions or principles which form the basis of the science."

Well, that's a load of, "Horseshit," everyone said.

"You'd think, with a job description like that,"

Marta said, "They'd have no trouble sitting bums in *World Summit* chairs."

We've gone around the mulberry bush a few times, contemplating Rule #6. There's a touch of political science in us all; we shouldn't be too smug or self-righteous. The essence of Rule #6 is simple: use your brain to make intelligent choices. Defining how "smart choices" are arrived at on-motorcycle in a split second is complex. If you're still baffled, here's a suggestion: find a Classic Biker and talk it through. Offer to polish their forks while your brain gets polished. Broaden your perspective. Your noggin will be better equipped to save you when it must make a life and death decision in half a second.

The cat's back. "Find anything tasty in the yard, Bunny? No? Well, let's get you some food then." Oh-my. My memory trigger has been, well... triggered. Sometimes the mechanism works too well. I can see bunnies being skinned alive. *There is more than one way to skin a cat...*

Tailor the Rules

"**A**BS FOR THE MIND," Marta calls the Rules. Once absorbed, Awareness and Ability are always on the job, never interfering with JOY. You may have to give yourself a metaphorical slap in the face occasionally to ensure your brain is on the job, but that's it: you can twist the throttle, ponder, and do all the things you love to do on your bike. Be an outlaw. Pull off the road and have sex, but not with a goat (more about sex and goats coming up). Scrape your pegs. Feel the rhythm of the road. Drop into one bend, accelerate out, and set up for another. You'll be tempted to quit your job and keep riding. What's over the next hill, I wonder? Let's find out.

Deserts have rolling hills with uneven surfaces instead of confined smooth blacktop like parking lot schools. There are no cones to avoid and no need to wear a high-vis vest. No instructors standing around with clipboards making judgment calls. There are natural berms to jump, hills to climb, and learning opportunities galore. Killers have nowhere to hide. The riding surface is forgiving if you go down. No gear pressure; blue jeans, a long sleeve shirt, sneakers, and an open-face helmet with a sunshade will do. A way to carry water is all the luggage required. I graduated when I was comfortable flying fearlessly, at full throttle toward a berm to achieve maximum air.

In Middle Eastern City there's an unwritten law—the police throw the book at expats regardless of fault. Foreigners in vehicles are always in season. It's part of the pact you agree to in exchange for living abroad. Here Rule #3 has a subclause: *You're always at fault, you foreign imperialist pig-dog. Pay up! Or else!* Generally, it's unwise to choose, or else. But if you're on a large 125cc, highly maneuverable bike, possess desert riding skills, and don't comprehend what's going on, do you ride like there's no tomorrow? Past the musallah where the adhān bellows from a speaker on the minaret of a mosque. You've watched the movie, *The Great Escape*?

Is it a wonder I eventually took to Curmudgeonly Jackassism? My parents tried to do the right thing, attach me to religion, but it didn't take. I wasn't keen on spending Sunday mornings dressing up, listening to hymn music, or kneeling. Motorcycle Church would have been a far better option—*everyone on their tidler. Open your books at Rule #4—n*o kneeling or preoccupation with sins and damnation. Sunday School on the Road to Joy.

Church works for many people. Curmudgeonly Jackassism works for me: no services, collection boxes, crusades, jihads, lousy music, and no rules about not using technology, like motorcycles. Bob and I used to joke about this being one of our teachings; "The Truth is out there." We stole it from the X Files.

When I told Marta, she said, "Yeah, but you jackasses won't find it." The rest of the teaching goes, "Buried under a rock." It's kinda like *Buddha lives in the circuitry of your bike*, except with a rock. Deep, right? We laugh when we say it, which isn't often because Asses don't hold regular services. It's an Absurdism. Most religions take theirs very seriously. *Mess with the word, and we'll chop your hand off!* Chill out. Get a bike. Go for a ride (and don't come back, religion-cunt).

I've never clued Marta in about where the rock is buried. She thinks we don't have a clue where the Truth is.

Remember my idea about motorcycles being mandatory for world leaders? Let's extend it to include religious leaders. Talk about getting closer to God; jump on a Husqvarna, Kawasaki, Vespa, or any bike. Peace on Earth through motorcycling! God be with you and with your motorcycle. Exodus 19:1-25. God called Moses up Mount Sinai and gave him the Ten Commandments *after he parked his dirt bike*. Stop looking for the ark. Use a metal detector and find the divine dirt bike. God only provided half a tank of gas. Moses couldn't have gone far.

There is no need to include Curmudgeonly Jackassism in the religious decree; most of us ride and are busy looking for Truth under a rock.

Religion is a big deal in Middle Eastern City. So is traffic, slaughtering lambs on side streets, and swindling naïve travelers. Car drivers deal with the congestion by flashing their headlights and honking their horns incessantly. Lambs don't comprehend they're on their way to becoming kebobs and tune out the craziness.

Fathers carry their wives, kids, chickens and a goat on their mopeds—the physics of moped loading is incomprehensible. I never understood how they managed, but it was clear Middle Eastern City families had a lot to lose. For them, Rule #1 was: *Everyone is out to kill me, my family, and my next meal.* Inshallah, God willing, it won't happen.

It's OK to tailor the rules to suit specific circumstances, like being a moped dad. Don't be blindsided because you didn't apply the rules to your situation. So, for example, you could expand #2 to remind yourself of a particular vulnerability: Don't Kill Yourself by Doing Something Stupid *like riding home from the bar, you pathetic drunken idiot!*

Tailoring isn't a rule, but permission to adapt. Dr. Li said, "It's nice that bikers have taken an affirming perspective." I was thrilled she liked my Tailoring Trigger and changed her mind about me being a Neanderthal. Here's how this one works:

1. Turn on a TV news channel;
2. Wait no more than four minutes;
3. A sexual rights story will air;
4. When it does, the name Taylor Templeton pops into my frontal lobe;
5. Sometimes an image of Taylor getting pounded also appears (both scenarios);
6. My brain makes the connection; it's okay to Tailor the Motorcycle Riding Rules.

Before it became trendy, Taylor Templeton jumped out of the blue and out of the closet. Today my brain

RULE #6, CHOICES   85

automatically links the sexual rights revolution to
Taylor, an easy Tailoring Trigger. "You see how you
can put an old, ingrained injustice to good use, Dr. Li?"
I'm pretty sure Dr. Li would say I've taken memory
trigger therapy to a whole new level.
See how simple it is to concoct MRR triggers?

The Truth About Sex and Motorcycles

Motorcycle Mommas, rampant outlaw rape,
and pillaging parties are relics of a by-gone
era. Some would say, "Too bad," but the fact
is, most motorcyclists are not misogynists, maso-
chism, rapists, sadism, anti-liberation Neanderthals.
Instead, we suffer from the same set of lust afflic-
tions as the clergy, senators, parliamentarians, steel-
workers, kindergarten teachers, and all humankind,
except Whirling Dervish Dancers. Marta agrees with
my position on motorcycles and sex but warns: I may
be influenced by "repressed Mary McGregor fantasy
baggage."
     She's probably right.
     I don't give a rat's ass if people are nonbinary, lean-
ing toward pansexual, a good old-fashion homosexual
like Taylor Templeton, or uncertain and experimenting. Just stop waving those holier-than-thou rainbow
flags and droning on and on about it, please. Look
at us; we're special and misunderstood nonhetero-
sexuals! No, you're not! That ship has sailed. Nobody

cares, so shut the fuck up! A custom chopper is special. You're not! We're busy trying to find the truth about motorcycles. You don't hear us droning on and on about it, getting endless media coverage, and winning gigantic financial settlements.

Because we're bikers, and no one gives a shit—it makes us strong.

If you're older and have scars, like Taylor, you're likely on drugs and sobbing in a corner, but if not, and you want to let loose, okay. Try to be brief and to-the-point. Also, buy a motorcycle and go for a long ride. It's the best possible therapy. Study the Rules first.

Are you opposed to same-sex shenanigans, and anything goes attitudes because of a deeply held religious belief? Fine by me. That's your prerogative. But keep a lid on it. Please! God will hear you out when it's your turn. Be patient. You'll be on deck right after followers of Curmudgeonly Jackassism, carrying the Truth we found buried under a rock.

Yes, the truth is out there, motorcycling is LGBTQ compliant. We have all your major persuasions covered. Dykes on Bikes, to name one well-known early adopter. Sure, we have sexual nay-sayers and our quota of deviants and predators; we're a diverse bunch. Everyone in the LGBTQ+ community is a saint, right?

Sexually frustrated? Buy a bike and go for a ride.

Truth About Motorcycles: Bikes don't care what adult sexual flavors their riders experiment with, off-motorcycle. There are more critical things to get feathers ruffled about when riding, like not getting killed.

Before I went globe-trotting, I secured an international driver's license. I thought it might impress the ladies.

Kidding!

I learned I'd need a snazzy bike to do that.

Off I went, into the congested playground of Nimrods, camels, donkeys, goats, and the odd snake, calling back over my shoulder to the few foreign spectators, "I'm not nuts! I'm a motorcyclist!" I could have added, "And a member of an increasingly LGBTQ+ compliant group, by the way." Young Middle Eastern City heterosexuals couldn't hold hands in public, let alone explore diversity. Want to lose your head over sex? Sometimes it's best to keep your mouth shut, your sex organs hidden, ethical positions in your back pocket, and always keep your motor running. You never know when you'll need to,

Scrape your pegs.

Goodbye TS-125

I hauled shopping bags of groceries, one dangling from each handlebar for balance, home to my apartment in Middle East City (I had yet to fully master Rule #2, Don't Kill Yourself by Doing Something Stupid). I toured, got out of the chaos for solo overnighters. No cell phone, tire repair kit, tools, GPS, luggage other than a backpack, or biker attire. TS-125, Mr. Dependable, never let me down despite my lack of gear and minimal language skills. Thank God! It didn't dawn on me then; motorcycles have problems that leave riders parked in Dire Straits. I was lucky to have an unbreakable, faithful companion. Otherwise, I'd have been deep in motorcycle do-do.

My circumstantial motorcycle training and development went well. Learning to ride, owning a bike that didn't want to kill me, Rule #1 locked in, and good luck brought me home intact. My rookie riding experiences were smooth as silk, with just enough frayed edges to teach me I had more to learn. Without knowing it, I lived the riding dream. Life is marvelous on two wheels! I fell in by complete accident, and everything slid into place. Not the bike, though; TS-125 stayed upright, no uncontrolled sliding. Despite my naivety, the motorcycle gods took care of me, guiding me onto the Road to Joy. I returned home whole, ready to nod knowingly when I read *Zen and the Art of Motorcycle Maintenance* for the first time. WOW! Robert nailed it!

I banked many riding years before Deadeye Dick locked GT in his sights and squeezed the trigger. Down I went.

Truth About Motorcycles: no one, including YOU, is immune to the rules that govern motorcycles.

PART 2: HOME AGAIN

RULE #7, BE STUBBORN

My riding euphoria came to an abrupt halt. I was motorcycle-less and uneasy. Sun and endless desert exchanged for west coast rain forest and deterrents, like family and mortgage. I dreamt of TS-125, but life turned that page. Thumper, as a replacement failed, the Killer left me mourning my old friend's MAGIC even more.

Here I was, listening to local biker chatter, trying to figure out why reasonable people, living in a miserable riding environment, bothered. Even stranger, *why are they fanatical about it? Don't they know any better? Riding in shitty weather, on roads, is not the Road to JOY. Am I missing something?* We swapped stories—Biker Conversation JOY. I offered a few TS-125 love stories. The riders were polite but dismissed my cheerful little machine as a toy. "Oh, you've never ridden a real bike," they asked? "Real" meant at least 500 pounds. Even Thumper wasn't a real bike. They owned large machines. Unlike riding in the desert, mass matters on the street.

They mostly swapped riders getting out of trouble stories, laughing off shitty weather, and the bull moose on the highway. The cop that nailed them, "but not at the speed I was doing a few minutes earlier!" I wanted to share my *soldiers in the shoot-to-kill pose followed by a die-you-foreign-pig-dog interrogation story,* but it seemed unrelatable in the rain forest. They talked of running out of gas and almost running out of gas. The semi that turned into their lane. Wind blasts on the plateau. The mattress lying on the road before the turnoff. Most of all, they looked forward to their next trip. I didn't know it then, but these veterans had developed a thick skin that allowed them to apply Rule #7:

Rule #7: Be Stubborn In A Good Way.

Never whine! Deal with consequences. Be Accountable! If Life, the Bully, targets you, become a soldier, like Hannibal, the original rider, who drove his elephant over the Alps and into war. Forward the Light Brigade! Two Wheels, Not Four!

Not even foul weather that keeps sane people indoors stopped my new friends. They spent fortunes on wet weather gear and heated grips, ventured out in less-than-ideal conditions, and found JOY. I thought this isn't right; I hadn't absorbed Rule #7.

Truth About Motorcycles: the Road to Heaven is Heaven; love the road you're on.

In the desert, #7 wasn't a big deal. It was easy going and going easy. The climate and terrain welcomed off-roaders. The predictably unpredictable traffic was a free-form small-bike maneuvering adventure. I was young and fit; I never had to tough it out, dig down to make the next stop. Listening to experienced western riders, I learned about new challenges, like miles of monotony, rainstorms, speed traps, bad gas, flat tires, gravel on asphalt, impenetrable traffic jams, deceptive corners, and risk management enforcement. Rational perseverance is your friend. Don't go off half-cocked with steam coming out of your head. That's Rule #2, Stupid. Avoid #2 by being Stubborn in a Good Way.

Truth About Motorcycles: maintaining balance on two wheels is critical.

Sometimes, the word "stubborn" makes me wonder if Bob flew into the Thompson River because he could. He could be bullheaded. *Bet I could fly halfway across the Thompson River. Kick-off my Lunar Rover Moonboots and swim out. Collect insurance, including new boot money.* Bob would say something like that but never do it. *Good plan, Bob. When you gonna do it?*

"What do you think, Bunny? Did Bob do it?" I'm not sure what happened to Bob?

Home with my pretty useless Desert & Chaos Motorcycle School Vaporware certificate, I read *Zen and the Art of Motorcycle Maintenance* for the first time, as well as *Jupiter's Travels.* I watched *The Long Way Down* and the *World's Fastest Indian.* Before Dicky loaded the Killer Bike rule into his sniper magazine, I dumped Thumper.

I drifted wide into Bike Lazy which led to a string of low budget, progressively larger street, It'll Do Bikes. I was moving on with my motorcycle education but still had a thing or two to learn. Three, to be exact if you're using the ten Motorcycle Riding Rules to count. But #7 was in my back pocket.

HAD TO BE THERE

Maybe a Zen master can define JOY, but I can't. For me, it's nebulous and rider-dependent (nevertheless, I may be stubborn in a good way, toss my ones and zeros out, and have a go at it in book two). The JOY Extreme Ape Hanger Guy feels does not flow from the MAGIC Rosie discovered in Pink Lady. JOY can be the serene peace of a comfortable, steady ride on a long, picturesque road; warm sun and cool breeze with a cold beer waiting at the end of the day. It may be skillfully scrambling up a hill, riding toward decaying ruins, or sighting a camel formation, like a caravan of old, or leaning into a curve, scraping cruiser pegs, or accelerating out on a sports bike.

Truth About Motorcycles: JOY calls
riders, and they climb on.

The clock ticks on. At this time in the narrative, I'm no longer alone–now I'm sharing life with my two kids, a cat, as well as my wife, Dori. The sprawling desert of exploration and rider training has gone; so, has cheerful little TS-125. Now all I have is yet another in a string of mediocre bikes. It'll-Do-Bike, better than no bike at all, but it would never be the gorgeous red Ducati in the poster stapled to the garage wall behind it. I wonder if It'll-Do-Bike was embarrassed? Thoughts of revenge, *I'll become a Killer Bike!* What if I'd stapled a Mercedes coupe poster behind the shitty, dented family sedan?

It'll-Do-Bike never tried to kill me, but neither did it form a Zen-like machine-human bond. In short, I became a Part-Timer; the sad decline of a former glory.

These are the things that turn motorcyclists into part-timers: familial responsibilities; the steady march of time that makes hours on the bike a bit uncomfortable; work, life speeding up, leaving less time for JOY; the bike you have that is only OK. Oddly, wild lunch-hour discussions about the cross-continent odyssey we planned to do one of these years had the opposite effect. Instead of riding more, we rode less, as if banking time for the dream trip; just heading out for a Saturday afternoon jaunt felt somewhat pathetic after watching *The Long Way Down*. Why bother? May as well save up for the epic ride. The more chatting we did about our grand adventure, the more we stayed put at home. When you're young, all-or-nothing attitudes persist. They gradually wear down to; just a bit will do.

"We" were a makeshift group—five workmates loosely bonded by motorcycles and corporate culture. Riding was a luxury; we should all have been working, mowing lawns, getting in shape, taking the kids to soccer, changing the oil in the van, fixing that loose tile in the bathroom, repaying Aunt Edna that overdue loan, taking a course, or bonding with our partners. We didn't get out on our bikes much—we were trapped, not in charge of our time. But Life, the Beautiful occasionally painted pictures of freedom and escape, tempting us.

Our low-budget, ok-but-not-great machines waited, lonely and ignored, left undercover or in the garage to collect dust for most of their days. They remained like statues, reminders of past glory. "Why don't you sell that thing? We could buy a carpet cleaner." Once a year, for three glorious days of summer, we'd make our move, like on the TV show *Prison Break.* Sometimes successfully. Often compromised.

We'd loosen the bonds, throw off the shackles of responsibility and take off on a brief but monumental ride—an abridged odyssey. Eagerly anticipating our parole, we'd cash in our Get Out of Dodge cards (the riding would be good, but escape is fantastic) and plan our adventure. Brush up on the Motorcycle Riding Rules, at least the ones we were familiar with. Up would roll the garage doors with the sunlight spilling in to show just how much grime the garage and our bikes had collected. As I sat wiping the dust off my bike, my thoughts drifted to Peter Fonda and Dennis Hopper in the 1969 movie *Easy Rider*–like them, I was heading off across America. Just without beautiful drugs. Or the proceeds from cocaine sales. Technically, we were in British Columbia, not America, and only going partway across one province. So, not like *Easy Rider* at all. But, motorcycles can transport you from one reality to another, like boarding a jet and stepping off on the other side of the world.

Our escapist, eclectic group of riders assembled. We wrapped our legs around steel like TV cowboys. Our two-wheelers polished and snug between our thighs. *Nicer than your average It'll-Do-Bike*, we fooled ourselves. In our minds, we were freedom fighters, but everything about us shouted "Part-timers!" A motley crew of weekend warriors with slapped together, bungy-corded luggage and makeshift riding gear that Beemer Bunch, with their superior machines and perfectly accessorized gear, would snub their noses at. Our bikes were as makeshift as our gear: an older Harley, a variety of Japanese brands and styles–nothing matched. Not credible enthusiasts, having made minimal investments in second-rate technology.

Except for Ninja Guy. No braces for his kids because he has no kids. No alimony either–you guessed it: he never married. With dollars to spare, he'd done his research and splashed the cash on a formidable machine that wouldn't hold back. Looked like he'd stepped off a motorcycle billboard. He was a threat to be taken seriously. A student of Physics Rule #3, regularly attending track days, camouflaged within a pack of part-timers, Ninja Guy would do our talking. "Look at him go! No one takes Ninja Guy. He's with us," we'd shout from our It'll-Do-Bikes. Truthfully, though, the rest of us didn't care: part-timers out for an escape, not a race, oblivious to motorcycle envy and neurosis. You tell yourself that because you know It'll-Do-Bike doesn't like to race, you could do something stupid or find yourself on a Killer Bike. Just wait till I get the red

Ducati in the poster on my garage wall!

*Truth About Motorcycles: JOY can't
be bought. It doesn't have a problem
with It'll Do Bikes or crappy gear.*

Day One, we travelled east, away from the coast
and over mountains that fell to rolling grasslands
and ended as desert. Not the arid, barren desert I
had trained in, with its hard-packed sand, but one
covered with sparse, low-growing shrubs and divided
by barbed wire fencing. So, we rode on a ribbon of asphalt down an endless highway.

Perfect weather: sunny and com-
fortably hot. Three o'clock put us an
hour from our planned overnight
stop. There would be beer, a meal,
some exploring, and many tall tales.
We rode through orchard country,
past fruit stands, gradually des-
cending into the valley where roads run beside long
deep warm water lakes. Apples, peaches, apricots, and
cherries. We looked forward to climbing off, resting
our bodies, snacking on fresh cherries, drinking beer,
reliving the day's ride, joking about the discomfort
of cherry diarrhea, and talking about how Ninja Guy
smoked the poser on the white and black bike.

We traveled under a blue sky, but a rebellious
storm waited in the distance. Ominous darkness
threatened to engulf us. It became a race—would we
make our motel before the menace in the sky caught

us and let loose on our shitty make-do, probably not water-resistant, Dennis Hopper outfits? We sped up. It was the best strategy we could come up with.

The storm appeared lost, out of place. It was not in our plan, meticulously scheduled to coincide with good weather, but there it was, a small renegade developing weather system, surrounded by bright blue summer skies. We were ill-prepared for the unpredicted looming battle.

The dark sky faded on each side, from black and threatening to light and inviting. We couldn't tell what was behind it, so we rode on a collision course with what was visible.

It began with thunder. It shook the ground, causing vibrations to radiate up through steel frames. Our thighs and legs pressed the machines, absorbing their strength. We leaned forward, closer to the bars. High energy bolts of lightning followed. We moved in awe toward this spectacle of nature, not twenty miles west of its grandeur. The sky exploded; it was otherworldly and indescribable. The motorcycles made us vulnerable participants. We rode toward nature's power in front row seats, marveling and fearing its consequences. There was no alternative but to continue, fully exposed but drawn toward the wonder of Life, the Beautiful.

We rode for twenty minutes, feeling the power and the glory, watching the orphaned storm, knowing God's hand touched Earth. There could be no other explanation; Awe replaced JOY.

Then the rain began. Warning drops at first,

quickly turning into a downpour. We persisted, ready to tough it out, to be stubborn in a good way. Just after the rain began, a fruit stand with a covered seating area miraculously appeared like an oasis in the desert. The store was decades old, always waiting by the road in the same spot. It was as it should be, but it seemed magical.

We climbed off, shaken. We had been moved by our shared experience, bombarded by, and amazed by nature's performance. No hugs. We didn't break into a chorus of Kumbaya or swear in an excited, exaggerated way about what we'd experienced. We were biker dudes.

We waited in silence, strong men. Bikers. Part-time outlaws. In the hands of God. Our It'll-Do-Bikes and make-do luggage tested by His storm or whatever you ascribe the realization that *there must be something more.*

Truth About Motorcycles: they can
reveal a glimpse of God.

After ten minutes, kickstands up; we rode to our motel under clearing skies, giddy kids, a band of brothers unified by an extraordinary phenomenon, one we'd never be able to share with others in a way that would do our hour of Awe justice. The encounter renewed my affection for motorcycles. It didn't matter that our bikes were shitty or that we were part-timers. Our machines made the experience possible, and we thanked them for it. It wasn't about skill, technical capability, or money; it was about being exposed, open to the Hand of God. It was one of those rare events impossible to describe. "You had to be there, "one of us would say."

The others would nod, yup, "had to be there."

And there's the rub of it: you had to be there. Sometimes you go for a ride and JOY finds you; once in a while, a trip leaves a memory that refuses to die, and these offset the drudgery that motorcycling can be. So, we ride, understanding the importance of being Stubborn in a Good Way.

Truth About Motorcycles: you have to be there.

Stubbornness means living with the reality waiting for you as you step off your motorbike because all trips inevitably end, and life naturally picks up where you left off. There is joy in daily living as well—I love my family. But now and then, I sneak down to where my garaged It'll-Do-Bike rests and stare adulterously at the red Ducati poster. Have a beer and dream about owning the road with Ninja Guy. Kitty always sneaks in to purr and provide advice about the importance of being mellow.

I look at It'll-Do-Bike and smile. *You remember, right? You were there. We share a bond now, It'll Do-Bike and me.*

Every road can be an adventure. I understand why people love to ride in their environment, whatever it may be, even if it's not on their dream machine.

I never owned the red Ducati in the poster, but I have had more extraordinary moments, sandwiched between hours of Motorcycle Tedium.

Truth About Motorcycles: JOY
and Tedium are mates.

Doldrums

The Oil Years followed the It'll Do Years. Oil is part of the default Biker Vocabulary, like, "how you likin' this weather? How about our sports team?" When you run out of subjects, the question is, "how you likin' that new oil?" Or, "you think'in of going full synthetic?" These are the conversations of the Oil Years. Nothing much happens. "How you likin' your new boots? Which oil filter you use 'in? Wax or sealer? Mid-grade or high octane?" The doldrums.

When my kids were approaching adulthood, I bought a used BMW R 1100RS. I figured it was time for something more than, It'll Do. That's how I met Bob. "Top speed, 140mph," were the first words out of Bob's mouth. If he'd asked, "what oil you use'in," maybe we wouldn't have hit it off?

Bob was on his V-Strom 650 and was thinking of trading it in. "Maybe on an RS." He liked the idea of "getting to know an oil head boxer." He also owned a big Japanese cruiser.

We became motorcycle buddies only because I owned the bike Bob had his eye on. Had I been riding my Concours at that time, we wouldn't have hooked up. Bob wasn't gregarious, and I'm socially lazy. We didn't have kids who played on the same sports team, similar occupations, nor did we live in the same neighborhood. But, we clicked—a couple of Asses.

Mostly we talked motorcycles, sometimes Bunny and Trident. Oil at times, though we were not passionate.

I think of my teal R 1100 and Bob as a pair, introduced to both simultaneously; they helped me emerge from the Doldrums.

Like TS-125, special bikes come along from time to time and fit perfectly at that moment in time. Teal RS was one of them. It was a coming-out bike—out of stagnation. Fortunately, I'd brushed up on Rule #3 (physics) because RS liked to race. Looking back, I was fortunate Deadeye didn't nail me— I pushed my luck on Teal Beauty.

I continued to ride happily until the crash, several bikes after R 1100RS.

PART 3: THE LOTTERIES

RULE #8, YOUR NUMBER

I often see lottery winners on TV holding up over-sized cheques: perplexity, confusion, and delight written large across their faces in equal measure. "I'm going to give up my shitty job and travel!" they shout at the interviewer.

I yell back, "And buy a bike, idiot! Even better, buy me one and I'll come with you. Don't forget to bring your credit cards."

Winning big lotto money is al-ways unexpected. That ticket, bought along with a small bag of peanut M&Ms, and gas, just like the hundred times before. Except on this day, despite enormous odds, the numbers came up. It was "out of the blue!" winners loudly remind the interviewer on the obligatory TV promo spot.

Would you please stop shouting! The interviewer puts on an, *I'm so happy for you,* professional smile. *Tickled pink!* The question that perplexes the inter-viewer is: Why do assholes always win? *Trying to make*

me feel bad, are you? Always the interviewer. Never the winner.

Well, Mr. Interviewer, the saints are busy saving the world. Gamblers win, not do-gooders or active adventurers. They don't have time to squander buying lotto tickets.

Dumb question, Mr. Interviewer: "were you surprised?" Of course, they were–the odds of winning are astronomical, and it's not like they did anything to help themselves. The Henderson's would have been overjoyed to win a free bag of M&Ms. I know I would; it beats the cheap Chester's Locks promo key chain I won ten years ago.

Sometimes I hear, "I do love my job and my colleagues and my little desk and the potted plants by the toilets, so I'm gonna keep working. What would I do if I didn't work?" WTF? Why did you buy a lotto ticket if you don't want change? *Has the world gone mad?* Brain's first thought always should be, MOTORCYCLE. Buy one to go with your peanut M&Ms. And then, buy me one. I'll show you the way and lend you a copy of *Scraping Pegs*. But no Horseshit! Keep up, pack your own gear, and don't whine!

As a famous actor once said: "Life is like a box of chocolates: you can always purchase a motorcycle and a copy of *Scraping Pegs* and head off on an epic adventure." Yes, he really said that. Or was it Marta at the lab? I remember Steven Wright, the comedian, once made this observation, "When everything is coming your way, you're in the wrong lane." He virtually quoted Rule #8.

Rule #8: Your Number May Come Up

Having the greatest day ever? Doesn't matter. With Rule #8, when they reach for your number, there's duck all you can do about it. No time to duck. It's Motorcycle's Dirty Little Secret.

Dirty Little Secret

The Motorcycle Lottery is not organized like the club door prize draw where they make a big production out of gathering everyone together to give away swag at a specific time. 7:30 PM—you're staring at the number on your red ticket, hoping to win the coveted key chain from Chester's Locks. "Everyone, check the number on your red ticket. Red tickets only. Who's going to be our lucky winner tonight? Let's give Chester, from Chester's Locks, a big hand for his generous donation."

There's always a NimRod who shouts, "Got it! On my blue ticket!" forcing the emcee to declare him a loser, which upsets Chester, who was trying to win customers, not piss them off.

If the Motorcycle Lottery were like the club door prize draw, you'd hear, "Okay, riders, jump on and go. Dicky will do the honours and pick one of you bastards off. Who will our unlucky winner today?" Here are the facts:

The Motorcycle Draw is always Under
the Table and Out of the Blue.

That's the deal with Motorcycle's Dirty Little Secret: people know it exists, but it's vague and meant for someone else. The industry likes to keep it on the down-low and the hush-hush, like Nazi extermination camps.

Usually, there are bits of the other rules mixed in with Rule #8, especially #1 (Everyone is Trying to Kill You)—lady runs a red light, blows a tire, and crosses the center line to hit you head-on. Sometimes it's out of a horror movie—those unsecured pipes falling from the flatbed in front of you, the open utility hole cover, or getting caught in the cross-fire of road rage. The key differentiator is speed; Rule #8 happens so fast, you're unable to take effective evasive action, so Deadeye's shot is a certainty. It's this simple: to climb on a motorcycle is to enter the draw. The ticket's free, and no one is excused. Not even Mr. or Ms. Really Expert Rider, who believe they're exempt. Timing is a mystery. Calamity always comes *out of the blue.*

When you pick up your bike at the dealership, the salesperson doesn't say, "And here's your free lottery ticket. Hope you don't win!" Nope, it's all about wind against your new helmet and the JOY that awaits down the neverending highway. Marketing types constantly suppress Motorcycle's Dirty Little Secret, but you know it's there. Don't you? Maybe around the next bend or right in front of Chester's Locks or just before Truth knocks you out?

Squabble

T hanks to Marta, there was push-back on #8's validity. "How can an event which a rider has no control over be a rule? A tire flies off a Mach truck. Nails a bike like a torpedo. That's a rule? C'mon! It's out of the blue, and there's bugger all to be done about it. Can't be a rule. It will undermine MRR's integrity."

I understand her skepticism. At least she didn't call it horseshit.

What is a rule anyway? A rule is an instruction you follow—it guides your behaviour. I can hear you thinking, indeed if you weren't thinking it, you should have been: I've struggled with this question myself because, as Marta stated, "#8 is fate, not a law." So, let's explore this seed of doubt.

As I rolled toward Salt Lake City, #8 was on my mind. *Out of the blue*, Brain stepped up in Wyoming. Long motorcycle rides are perfect for resolving perplexing questions.

I also had other matters to consider, not just the integrity of #8. Occasionally I put Marta's challenge aside to wonder, will I find Aprilia's and Harleys parked at the Tabernacle and witness Mormons on bikes? If so, Joseph Smith and the Church of The

Latter-Day Saints might be onto something. Does the *Book of Mormon* contain answers not revealed in the *Zen* book?

Ok, truth time–I wasn't committed to investigating the Mormon–cycle proposition, but I pondered the possibility on my long ride. Eventually, I decided, fuck it! Good enough just to see the Tabernacle. No need to explore faith's connection to inanimate objects. I'm no Robert M. Pirsig. Mormons on bikes is a dusty detour but *worth a quick look while I'm there.*

Full honesty: I wasn't traveling all that way to see the Tabernacle either. I was going to the 2017 MOA BMW rally, not on a mission to investigate the symbiotic interaction of man, God, and motorcycles, just going to take part in a two-wheel cultural-commercial exposition. Like Sturgis cut with water, starch, and German Königsberger Klopse. Now that is God's Truth. I figured; I'm in SLC, may as well take in the big church as one does.

That's all there was to it; I really was traveling across the grasslands when I alternately contemplated #8's validity, and do Mormons ride? Now that I recall the trip, I was also dreaming about the tasty cowboy breakfast in the town of Rock Springs. Drop by if you're in the area; you know where to go now. I did, and what a brilliant decision!

That's all there was to it. In a nutshell, I was riding toward Utah to reach SLC and attend the MOA rally. Full confession, the rally was merely an excuse to hit the road. I barely "attended." Basically, I needed a break from Marta's constant badgering about #8. She can be so tenacious. And that's why I had plenty of time to think.

Over a thousand miles in the saddle, you know what it's like? The excellent morning meal in the town of Rock Springs also replayed in my mind. I was getting #8 straight in my coconut, taking my time, enjoying the coffee, then a second cup. When I considered a third cup, it hit me–I was stalling. Not that I was afraid–heck, no, I love biking; I love it so much I'm writing a damn nonfiction book about it instead of the one Marketing wanted, filled with outlaws, whores, and crashes (just one crash). No, what I mean is that the prehistoric medulla-hypo-meta-whatever in my brain unconsciously realized that I would drop back into the Motorcycle Lottery when I left the café and got on my bike. So, my number may come up. Since the cafe was cozy, the breakfast tasty, and the coffee strong and sweet, my primal brain urged me to keep my ass safe and secure in the chair. That's the thing about dirty little secrets. They often like to poke up and remind you; you can't hide under the covers forever.

Eventually, I climbed on and tore off. The medulla-hypo-meta-whatever in my brain settled down. I enjoyed a moment of Absolute Clarity.

Since my stalling was a behavior, from our earlier definition that rules guide behavior, #8 must be a rule! Hallelujah! No wonder the folks at MRR Labs eventually listen when I orate. It's not simply because I oversee Marta's snack budget, as Earl said.

I was so excited; I almost wheeled around and

pointed my bike back to Rock Springs for a second celebratory Cowboy Breakfast, but the travel allocation (from Larry's donation) was running low, so I didn't. "Capital preservation," the financial folks call it.

I pulled over and crunched a battered pickle instead.

I can hear philosophy graduates applauding my logic; the motorcycle engineers vociferously disagreeing while insisting #8 remains pure random chance and demeans the value of logical rules. "Why don't you just attach a roulette wheel to your rule book?" I respect their point of view, sort of, and agree to disagree. I asked the PolSci crew working at the fast-food place for a second opinion. Last we spoke, #8 had triggered a heated exchange on the potential discriminatory effect of male-generated rules in a pluralist society. Whatever that means? Hello, right brain to planet Earth. But they were able to serve a barely edible chicken sandwich.

My defense of #8 continues: behavior is affected before the rule comes into effect, but also afterward. You're riding along, thinking, the world is my oyster, and it happens, *out of the blue*. Whamo! Your number comes up. Suppose you're dead, which is twenty-six times more likely in a motorcycle accident than a car accident, end of the story. If you're not dead, there are years of painful physical rehab, counseling for panic attacks, feeding your free PTSD service dog, and the loss of friends as you retreat to your bedroom and discover the local dealer delivers. Sure, that's the worst case, but either way, #8 affected your behavior. Rules influence behavior; remember the definition?

You may agree with the motorcycle engineers and label it "tittle-tattle and fuddle-duddle." Still, my Wyoming decision stands: Your Number May Come Up remains a rule, cemented in the eighth position. And scrub those suggestive, *where I can shove #8*, scribbles off the MRR Labs unisex garage washroom wall! Charge the cleaning supplies to the Snack and Washroom Maintenance Budget. I won't be reallocating money from my travel budget, Marta!

More Discord

M arta is a very smart cookie, but sometimes I feel like poking her in the Guzzi.

With reluctance, Marta eventually smartened up. "Your Number May Come Up can be a rule, albeit somewhat of a lameo." But, like my cousin Lenny, Marta doesn't know the meaning of *silence is golden*.

For the love of God, Marta. Enough already! "What's that?"

"You heard me. Why's it #8? Due to its finality, it must be the last rule… out of respect for common sense and order! Your number comes up…finito! No need for more rules! Your goose is cooked. Full stop. Did you throw a dart at a board to arrive at #8's position? Talk it over with a bovine in Montana?"

"Glad you asked, Marta."

Actually, I wasn't pleased; Marta can be a pain. Robert M. Pirsig would never have finished his maintenance book had Marta been around to badger him. Ditto for Professor Hawking. "You expect me to believe that black holes just popped up *out of the blue*?"

Marta's position answer is simple: 8 provides hope of continuing toward 9 and 10. The two remaining rules wait like lighthouse beacons, spreading symbolic rays of optimism. To modify a well-known greener grass idiom: "the road is always curvier further on." There is evidence of survival beyond the blast site—former riders, living their decrepit lives, some with free service dogs. "Hope is so very important, Marta. That's why *Your Number May Come Up* is staying put where it is. In a word, HOPE."

"Battered pickle?" So, like Marta to change the subject.

"Makes sense," right?.

Die Tryin'

W hen I won my Chester's Locks key chain, it occurred to me, maybe that's my number drawn and done with. I won a cheap promo chain instead of a billion dollars, but at least the odds of my number resurfacing are minuscule. Thank you, Chester and the lottery gods!

It proved not to be the case but,
Hope Springs, Eternal.

Not that I know where Eternal is, and aren't springs for damping? Or is the morning meal in Hope Springs better than that of Rock Springs?

HOPE is like a rosy visor flicked down to give everything a pleasant tinted glow. All is well, it says. Motorcyclists will not be browbeaten by Risk Management Guy or intimidated by the odds of going down. Even when Rule #8 fires from Deadeye's rifle, HOPE remains.

My cousin Len is a Motorcycle Lottery poster boy. A survivor. Although it's good Len's still around, one-legged but more than capable, the downside is he continually yammers on and on about his stub to anyone who'll listen, and boy, does Stumpy like to talk about how my fat auntie nailed his Yamaha. Just like some folks can't stop talking about war. By the way, it's nice that the Japanese and the Germans both did a 180 after WWII: their countries now produce excellent motorcycles, which spread JOY worldwide. "Don't forget the Italians," Marta adds.

I wonder if any motorcycles survived Hiroshima? If they did, were they safe to ride?

People say this about me; "You're about as empathetic as a lab rat. For a shoulder to cry on, I'm going down the hall to HR, where the caring folks hang out. You have no sympathy for one-legged cripples or Hiroshima victims." Wrong! Just because my sleeve says, *cry me a river asshole* rather than *compassionate warmth found here* doesn't mean I'm cold-hearted. Ever heard of strong, silent, semi-Newtonian types? Remember, I own a cat? Bunny, and before that

Squirrely. And a dog? Pearly, and before her, Opal. I'm an Honorary Copley Park Dog Mom, for Christ's sake. Plus, I brought Len a potted plant when he was in the hospital. My sister Barb advised me, "I'm sure Lenny will appreciate a nice plant." He didn't. Didn't even ask what model it was. I was prepared; "Spider Plant." Guess he's not a deeply sensitive nature and animal lover like me. Plus, I'm against war and dropping bombs out of the sky—they may land on motorcycles.

There must be better ways for countries to develop motorcycle design and manufacturing expertise?

I must ask my cousin; did you ride long enough to feel JOY? The few moments of elation that keep riders climbing on? The vibrancy of the extraordinary mechanical beast beneath, twitchy and responsive; its proud parent-like engineers watching from the banked corner you've just nailed, saying, "we've done our jobs well." Or ambling along a serene country road. Maybe dodging a traffic jam feeling like a million bucks? JOY can happen anytime, anywhere. It's a product of uncaged wheels. Here's the thing:

Motorcycle JOY is what they call "nebulous." MRR Labs has been unable to pin it down, although we suspect it has to do with weather, the absence of car doors, twisty roads, no cops, little traffic, and superb engineering.

Lenny was a Blockhead. Doubt he made it beyond noisy pipes and *Born to Be Wild*. Too bad.

My friend, Larry's death, was joyless because he's one of those who went through life *motorcycle-less.* He wasn't even doing anything stupid the day he died. His sickly, depressed, fatso colleague stuffed down an entire box of Larry's crackers without a problem. He was so absorbed with his cracker binge; he didn't notice his business partner choking on a single seaweed cracker. When asked how it happened, fatso shrugged and said it was, "*Out of the blue*." I could never convince Larry to give motorcycling a try because "I don't want to die." But he did. Crackering. Nevertheless:

> *Don't encourage friends to take up motorcycling. They may win the Motorcycle Lottery. Then family members will torment you. Uncle Wacko may attempt to run you off the road.*

Guy Clark has a song called Die Tryin'. I like to think it's about Motorcycle Riding Rule #8. If a motorcycle takes you out, at least you died tryin'. If a cracker takes you out, well...

If you're alive, you're in the Death Lottery, and like Larry, your number may come up served on a cracker. It works the same way as the Motorcycle Lottery, but it's not a Dirty Little Secret. We expect to die. Nevertheless, like the people of Hiroshima, it can come as a shock. Animals are blessedly off the hook. Otherwise, life would be a giant holocaust for many of them. Instead, they ride the slaughter truck to the abattoir thinking, Life is Beautiful.

You can't withdraw from the Death Lottery, but the Motorcycle Lottery? Dump your bike and buy a low emission tank. Or stay in bed. But remember, shit happens in tanks, on beds, and in Hiroshima too. Drop by the garage; I'll walk you through Marta's flowchart. It does an excellent job illustrating how everything ends in Death, but not all Life Paths create JOY.

It's a safe bet the same outfit operates both the Motorcycle and Death Lotteries. The draws often work sequentially. Number comes up in the Motorcycle Lottery, and there's a good chance you'll kick the bucket. Another mystery in need of resolution, who runs these lotteries? Start your search at the Tabernacle in SLC. Or at the Vatican. Mecca? Or Lotto Central? Rock Springs? It doesn't matter, but please get on it. When I looked, I didn't find any Illuminati, just a bike shop selling those LED driving lights that are way too bright. Actually, I wasn't looking—just another lame excuse to go for a ride on the Lab expense account. The travel form Marta created requires "Purpose of Trip" to be filled in.

Lottery timing is an enigma, although if you're ninety-six, had a heart attack, have no health insurance, and were wheeled into the boiler room next to the morgue, it's a safe bet; your number is coming up. Same thing: if you're cranked up on Bennies, don't have MRR, and decide to see if your friend's Panigale will do 130 mph / 210 km per hr.

Let's wrap this up. We've beaten Rule #8 to death with a stick. We accept its validity because:

Behavior. I've laid out how #8 can modify behavior. Yes, it's a metaphysical argument, and motorcycle engineers aren't on side, but too damn bad. Political science supports my position.

HOPE. There is a reasonable chance you'll come out of the Motorcycle Lottery, battered but alive and perhaps get a free service dog. Without HOPE, why bother learning the other nine rules? #9 and #10 provide anticipation of reaching JOY further down the road.

Preparation. Housekeeping is important. Use #8 as a reminder to ensure your insurance policy is paid up, your underwear is laundered, your will is up to date, and generally to do those things referred to as polishing your gravestone.

JOY. Thanks to Rule #8, taking care of business will allow you to ride easy, knowing you've done everything possible. It's in God's hand. There is nothing more to do except cruise over to Rock Springs for the Cowboy Breakfast.

PART 4: HEADING OUT

RULE #9 & 10, GOATS

I left home, Victoria, British Columbia on August 16, 2019, with my riding buddy, Conrad. Both of us on BMW F800 GTs, mid-sized touring machines. Mine, white with a small custom teal accent; Conrad's, dark graphite. We were experienced riders; older, not stronger, skilled but trying not to be complacent, a bit slower to react but not as impatient. To compensate, we had both moved to smaller bikes. The F800s are forgiving; they have the knowledge of generations engineered into them. They know a thing or two about what to do and what not to do. Put a competent, experienced rider on a capable bike, and you'd think the odds of their number coming up would be minuscule. Especially ones who have MRR in their back pockets. But as they say, you only need one ticket to win.

On I climbed and into the draw I went.

Between us, we had over fifty years of injury-free riding—a couple of bumps and scrapes, but nothing dramatic. A year earlier, Conrad was attacked by a wild turkey on the American plains —a duct tape and tie wrap repair job got him home. His number came up and he won a shitty prize. The unfortunate thing is, Rule #8 doesn't go on hiatus. My buddy remained in the draw.

Turkeys and roundabouts can be irritating (remember Movie Bike)? A single irritant like hot, oppressive weather or a buzzing monster caught in your helmet can piss all over your state of mind. In your madness, you make stupid happen. You get the idea, so here's Rule #9:

Rule #9: An Irritant May Get Your Goat

Rule #9 has implications beyond the apparent meaning that "to get your goat" is "to drive you mad or cause you to flip out." The hidden, the silent, sardonic

 part is... *And the Goat Will Kill You!*

A #9 Killer Goat is like a chunk of kryptonite; suddenly, you're on your knees, and #9 is bunting the hell out of you. An irritant triggers another rule, and it's goodbye yellow brick road. Repercussions. Rules interact. One thing leads to another. Radical Dick taps his brother on the shoulder, "I've had it with this duck. He's getting my goat. You're a better shot, Deadeye." Dicky raises his sniper rifle and fires. Thanks to Radical, another duck down.

Marta illustrates all this in her flowchart. The diagram's a blessing for those of us who learn best with visual aids. It's almost finished. A nice donation to the Lab's Battered Pickle Procurement Fund may put it to bed.

Being asked to donate is irritating. Visiting the in-laws or Dr. Peggy is like letting a bug crawl under your skin. But in these examples, coping mechanisms such as heavy drinking, tapping, or Whirling Dervish dance are available. On-motorcycle, it's just you and your lonely noggin. Developing techniques to defend against Killer Goats isn't easy but it may save your life.

Never make things worse by climbing on after confronting Goats, bent out of shape over a bad relationship, who ate the last piece of carrot cake, whose turn it really was to change Bunny's litter box. Goats love pissed-off—it greases their way.

One irritant may be manageable, but two? Three? You bite your tongue while chewing gum, which hurts like hell, right after having the Cowgirl Breakfast you got talked into when you wanted the Cowboy Breakfast. That breakfast sits niggling in your stomach as you crawl behind the annual RV parade, right at the best section of the highway. Damn breakfast choice! Horrid gum! Bastard RVs! All the while watching the low tire pressure indicator and wondering if the next part of your day has you stranded with a flat. Finally, cracking through your disgust, you spot an opening and roar past the parade, smack into the side of an RV turning left into *Rendezvous in the Forest*. The gum caused you to bite your tongue, irritating the hell out of you. You did something stupid, and Rule #2 leaped up and bit you. Yes, more than one Killer Goat was involved; it's complicated.

RV turning out? Well, it... turns out... that a Goat blurred your vision, and you missed the *Rendezvous in the Forest* banners. Turns out that disgust started with a bitten tongue. Turns out, you shoulda let it go and got over it, but a Goat was pissing on you. Turns out, that one irritant got you good. If only you'd spit the gum out. The stupidity of biting yourself. And then More Goats piled on.

Let's clear the decks of Goats before carrying on. There's only one rule left, and we've touched on it already. So, we'll put them all on the table as Conrad, and I hit the road heading for the crash site. So here it is, the end of the list, for now.

Rule #10: The Multiplier Effect Is

Also Trying To Kill You

A single irritant (we all have an Achilles' heel) can pick a rider off. Often these mistakes or distractions are not huge deals in and of themselves, but they escalate, one on top of another. Frustration levels rise, and accidents happen. Don't tell Marta, but I added #10 to answer her nitpicking. She likes to go on about how all the rules work together, and I shouldn't single them out. "I believe you're talking about the Multiplier Effect, Marta. Rule #10."

One time, I forgot to put my magnetic tank bag on properly after gassing up. I was thinking about what an asshole my boss is. The bag came flying off and landed on the street when I pulled out of the station —a SQUID move, but not a game-changer. I put the kickstand down and went to retrieve it but tripped on the curb—another jackass move. I went sprawling. If you'd been watching, you might even have called it a decent-looking fall, as I did a tidy barrel roll when I landed, though I didn't appreciate scratching my helmet. But I rolled too far... and landed in front of oncoming traffic. Thankfully, it was moving slowly, but it had rained earlier, and the road was slippery. The nearest car saw me, slammed on its brakes, and skidded in slow motion towards me. I didn't have time to move and ended up with my hands on the hood, staring in semi-horror at the equally terrified driver. One foot more and I'd have been tackled. Five miles an hour faster, and the cars behind would have rear-ended him. As it was, they'd been able to stop in time.

The multiplier effect had kicked in, but luck was with me. I glimpsed DD laughing and wagging his finger, saying, "You can't always be so fortunate Jackass."

"Just wanted to retrieve my bag, Dick," I explained. "Must you always be so damn trigger happy?"

"It's what I do. My job. Part of the fabric of life. Me and my Goats."

Another time, one of my bugaboos happened: a large, pissed-off, stinging insect became trapped in my helmet, very much alive. It buzzed like a killer drone, unable to escape and extremely pissed-off. You would be too. Flying along, minding your own business, and suddenly you're sucked inside a stinky hell hole with no way out. My gloved fingers were useless. Panic levels rose as I waited for the creature to drill into a fleshy part of my head, perhaps my eyeball, blinding me. I was traveling at a good clip with nowhere to pull over. Barely under control. I'm not over the edge but teetering on madness despite the extreme threat level. Suddenly, there are other tasks to perform besides pest control. Passing. Braking. Signaling. A car over the center line. The multiplier effect was kicking in BIG time.

You should know: I escaped. I like to think it was because I practice Zen Jackassism and try not to let things get my goat. The Mexican Killer Bee, which it turned out to be, having eluded the southern border, had tangled itself in the padding of my helmet. I dodged the straying car, passed the slowing truck, signaled my intention to change course, and braked to a halt in a driveway. My heart was pounding faster than a Rush drum solo. Slowly, it returned to normal. So, I took my helmet off and flicked the killer away. Did Dick send it to distract me? Asshole!

That's what it's like with the Multiplier Effect. One manageable problem never causes a huge issue, not your kryptonite. But they can pile up, add together, and overwhelm. You lose the ability to control the situation for seconds, giving Deadeye a clear shot. The Multiplier Effect is one sneaky SOB.

When dealing with Goats, do the opposite of your initial reaction; don't twist the throttle and drive like a possessed Blockhead in an ill-advised attempt to out-run them. Instead, release the throttle, pull over, and let them wander off.

Congratulations!

HALLELUJAH!
Take a bow, dear reader, and soak in the applause. You've completed *An Introduction to MRR*. Now gas up, get on, ride out and end the day with JOY, sitting beside Buddha and the MAGIC of your machine, breathing fresh air and

thumbing through a copy of *Pegs* because repetition is essential.

If you're experienced, perhaps more experienced than me, you may be saying to yourself, fuck-off, I knew this stuff. *In fact, I know it all, have pretty much done it all, and don't need a jackass telling me how to ride.*

It's okay! I'm not offended. I wrote at the start, developing and maintaining your Motorcycle State of Mind (or whatever you choose to call it) is up to you. Biker magic al answers cannot be packaged. MRR may help some think, but in the end, each rider carries their cocktail of Awareness, Ability, and Accountability.

Although Marta has suggested offering seminars with a diploma, at this time, there are no MRR certificates, like the ones awarded Parking Lot Cone School graduates. "For an additional charge, take home a copy of the flowchart," Marta proposes. "Perhaps a free

battered pickle if we can work a deal with Tony's Deli."
Marta's always thinking.

The rules we covered are pretty straightforward,
right? Even the bits involving metaphysics, calculating atomic weights, and understanding dramatic license. Maybe you'll adapt, tailor, or make up a memory trigger or two? First, grab a drink and let loose
with Die Try'in or a John Prine song or whatever turns
your spokes because you're a Parking Lot Cone School
and a MRR Graduate!

Rejoice!

PART 5: THE CRASH

BORDER CROSSING

Conrad and I had logged thousands of uneventful motorcycle miles. No injuries. No unrideable bikes. Our young and daring days survived, now we were balanced, better equipped to smell the roses, and wait for appropriate stretches of road to demonstrate our knowledge of motorcycle physics.

Nothing much gets our goats anymore.

You're thinking, "nothing much" is secret code for a festering irritant sure to unleash a goat, result in calamity, and punch up a boring trip report. Is it a hint of a twist?

What is it about an innocent sentence that will immediately have readers suspecting there's more to this narrative than meets the eye? You're thinking: trouble brewing under the covers? A dirty little non-motorcycle secret? One of the guys has cancer? Will the two jackasses end a close friendship in fisticuffs at a truck stop wrestling match? Perhaps he's leaving the spouse... Is the spouse leaving him? Money problems? Pet to put down? Kid turned out to be a freak? Does Conrad secretly enjoy Brussels sprouts? Those annoying squeaky brakes? Who's turn is it to pay for coffee? A difference of opinion over pluralistic societies? Something is afoot. It's sure to get under their helmets and alert Mr. Dick. DD is always on the lookout, but you'd be wrong.

This is a non-fiction book, remember? Not *The Valley of the Dolls* or *The Scarlet Pumpernickel*. It's life, based on actual events. Reality with motorcycles, not nebulous black holes and no rules. Down to earth, unlike Steve's *Time* book, which takes place in the cosmos, wherever that is. Conrad and I were easygoing, going-easy, nothing getting our goats, no irritants floating by. No mystery novel subplots. Where's Bob? At home. I invited him, but he had a conflict and couldn't make it.

I should warn you, full disclosure: my number was coming up. And the prize would be more consequential than the key chain I won years ago. It wasn't "tits up" to use a trashy fiction novel term. Not all the way to the Final Destination, but certainly resting in the parking lot just outside the Valley of Death.

It's essential to be clear. Before you read about what happened, let me tell you again that absolutely nothing was interfering with the peace of this particular ride. It was one of those trips you'd describe as "smooth sailing," or "a walk in the park," or "nothing at all getting your goat."

The August weather was perfect the day we left. From the southern tip of Vancouver Island, a two-hour ride north to catch a ferry to the mainland, near Vancouver. We'd ridden the BC-Washington circle route many times. There would be no surprises, nothing we weren't prepared for, a laid-back cruise through spectacular scenery and varied landscapes. A routine getaway, not an odyssey. We were neither looking to find ourselves, explore a lost land in a far-off place, or morph into weekend outlaws. Just a short, pleasant cruise with a bit of scraping pegs along the way.

We added a few appropriate adjustments to the rules; nothing that would justify a committee review, just little extras, like *leave early, stop early,* and *don't eat at joints that serve Brussels sprouts.* Who said you can't have fun? This isn't a *Brief History of Time* with a complete absence of motorcycles. Yes, an academic book can be fun! It doesn't have to be *the sky is exploding! We're all going to fall down a black hole and implode!*

The ride up the island to catch the ferry is scenic, compensating for the strangle hold the risk folks have on the Island Highway. It's slow, full of cops, and littered with road safety improvements designed to prevent cager-idiots from killing themselves and bikers from scraping pegs. An hour and a half of ocean cruising, and we're on the mainland, the Sea to Sky Highway. As we passed Whistler Resort, host to winter Olympic ski events, I had a revelation. A moment of Absolute Clarity. Skiers fly down mountains, uncaged, going ninety miles per hour. They wear helmets, humongous boots, and special gear. Remind you of motorcycling?

Like riders, skiers deal with forces trying to kill them. Skiing and motorcycling are identical except for minor differences, like noise, athleticism, snow, and Boldness. So, why are these twin passions cultural opposites? Buddha hangs out in motorcycle circuitry but avoids ski boots? Where are the ski gangs and clubhouses filled with drugs and hookers? Do skiers not hit the slopes to get over horrific life problems? Is there a fringe helmetless ski movement? Why do nearly identical activities have such different personas?

Skiers will never figure it out. Even if they read the *Zen* book, they'll still be scratching their lame helmets. Motorcyclists have the immense advantage of jumping on Thinking Machines and riding until they have moments of Absolute Clarity. Skiers have pieces of carbon fibre epoxy strapped to their feet, gliding on snow that freezes their basal ganglia, preventing meaningful thought. Just before the town of Pemberton, BC, the distinction hit me: *Motorcycle riders are bold free thinkers. Far more open-minded than skiers. Skiers shelter in confined areas, on mountains, like bears, at certain times of the year. They have not evolved to the same degree as motorcyclists. Mr. Pirsig did his research and chose not to write Zen and the Art of Ski Waxing.*

It was worth passing Whistler to get this gem straight in my noggin, never mind the magnificent scenery. There may have been more cultural perceptions to unpack, but Conrad interrupted my pursuit of logic with an equally insightful comment, "We can stop at the next café for a bite. They don't serve Brussels sprouts, and I'm feeling peckish."

"Alrighty," I replied through the intercom. Do ski helmets have internal comms, I wondered?

The GTs wound through the snow-capped mountain valley, bordered by emerald lakes, to the start of a must-ride motorcycle highway. Highway 99, Pemberton to Lillooet, BC, known by locals as the Duffey Lake Road. It has magnificent scenery and a two-lane, twisting, old-fashioned, secondary highway to take riders from sea level, over mountains to the hot, dry interior. The perfect start to our four-day excursion. There was no need to remind each other; it doesn't get better than this!

There are secret must-ride roads scattered on every corner of the globe. They're confidential, so I can't be certain. Respect my Duffy Lake Road disclosure, please–don't get the locals up in arms! If I'm able to return to the Duffey Lake road one day, I don't want to see a sign that says: "No Jackasses!" because readers took it upon themselves to make a mockery of "secret." I don't want protestors outside my garage carrying this sign: "Thanks for Wrecking our Secret Road, Scraping Peg Assholes!"

Unlike Scotland's Secret Bunker, a widely known decommissioned nuclear command centre turned tourist attraction, now doing a tongue-in-cheek disservice to the word "secret," secret motorcycle roads are genuinely obscure. You are welcome to go to the Secret Bunker–it's now a tourist destination, the opposite of secret. The Scots will sell you a Secret Bunker coffee mug and a Secret Bunker tee shirt. Motorcycles welcome! Take a "I Visited the Secret Bunker" sticker for your Triumph. Warning: now that it's no longer in the nuclear business, you must pay to park. The lot wasn't a " revenue-generating opportunity " when the Newtonians ran it, but the Secret Bunker Marketing team changed that.

Scots wear kilts without boxers, drink scotch by the gallon, play a mean bagpipe, eat haggis, and deep-fried Glaswegian Mars Bars (yes, you can buy them at the Secret Bunker). Marta tried one and reported, "They could make a killing selling battered pickles." But Scot's true testament to Boldness was operating a nuclear command bunker. It's like waving a flag, "Over here, Mr. Nuclear Annihilation Dick!" Finito! Scotland.

Conrad flicked his indicator as I pondered the differences between secret motorcycle roads and secret nuclear facilities and placed Scottish Boldness ahead of Skier Boldness on my Top Ten Boldness List. Finally, we pulled into the *No Brussels Sprouts Café.*

The No Brussels Sprouts Café's disdain for the diminutive cabbage has nothing to do with the vegetable's disgusting taste or sickening skunk-cabbage odor. Stop by, and Barry, the owner, will regale you with the story of his Flemish ex-wife who ran off with a lady skier from Whistler. After your meal, remember, please do not proceed to the Duffey Lake secret motorcycle road! Turn your tails around and head toward Whistler and Vancouver.

"Back again, boys," Barry greeted us. "Care to try our No Sprouts, Just Tons of Butter Croissant?" So, we ordered two, with extra butter. "Sad news. My ex won the Ski Lottery. Still with us, but so very close."

August 17, the GTs stopped at a motorcycle rally in the postcard-perfect hot springs, lake-side Village of Nakusp, BC (also a great riding area but not a secret). We said our hellos, talked oil, and listened to rally gossip for an hour.

How to describe a biker rally? As a kid, I was disillusioned with scouting and became a dropout. Helping old ladies across streets, which scouting is very fond of pointing to as its raison d'être, screamed that Baden Powell didn't think things through well. Endlessly preparing for an impractical good deed that will never happen is stupid. Same goes for reef knots, and don't get me started on semaphore. When was the last time you used a reef knot on your motorcycle? Don't be a Luddite; buy those knotless straps. If Baden Powell had owned a motorbike, scouting would be a viable movement today. Motorcycles are much better at molding young minds than reef knots, Grand Howls, or experimenting with same-sex relationships.

A biker rally is the grown-up version of a Girl Guide or Cub Scout jamboree populated mostly with dropouts and the blacklisted. Just with more beverages, drugs, and grown-up socializing. Some legitimate badge decorated ex-scouts, converts to motorcycling, attend. You'll find them volunteering to tie reef knots for wayward campers.

Veterans of sleeping on rocks and listening to snores, we skipped the experience and carried on to the *Down and Dirty Motel*, further south. Affordable: we each had one of those rooms that make you shudder if the light is bright.

On the morning of August 18th, 2019, the bikes passed over the Canada - US border. Uneventful since Donald never insisted on erecting a wall or even a "Please Keep Off the Border" sign.

We crossed the border multiple times a year and were in the Homeland Security Computer (filed under *Jackasses?*). You two again? I had unconcealed contraband inside my top case. Why didn't they look? Pull me into the interrogation room and drill me about the illegal half-eaten bag of Canadian cherries I'd forgotten to throw out? When I most needed officialdom, it failed me. They're never *Johnny-on-the-spot where they're needed.* Exceed the speed limit by 7 mph on the salt flats and outcomes their gigantic cloud-based rule book to take giga-bites out of our bank account and suck the joy out life.

We arrived in Republic, Washington at midday, an hour and a bit south of the border. It was a scorcher, 90F/32C. Our reservation was in Omak, an hour and a half southwest. From there we would ride over the Cascade Mountains to catch a Washington State ferry back to Vancouver Island.

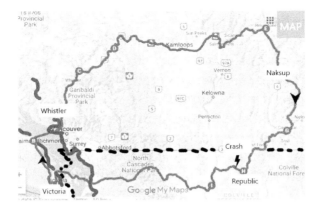

Our Planned Route

HORACE THE HORRIBLE

We pulled the F800s over in the town of Republic to kill time. Ahead of schedule, we didn't want to arrive at our motel before the three o'clock check-in. Our leave early stop early rule was problematic. Entirely Conrad's fault. He was leading. Ex-military. Understood the critical nature of time. Logistics expert, able to use the twenty-four-clock. I'm a Cub Scout flunky, for heaven's sake, focused on Marta's snack and washroom maintenance budget request; I couldn't be watching the clock as well. "Additional unbudgeted responsibilities." Marta was beginning to sound like a government bureaucrat. Request denied!

Just after we crossed the border, I asked myself this question: if Steve had included a song in his book, would it be Cyndi Lauper's *Time After Time* or The Chamber Brother's *Time Has Come Today*? I suspect Steve is a secret Brit rocker, and the Rolling Stone's *Time Is on My Side* would be up for consideration. With questions like this to resolve, was I supposed to be paying attention to Greenwich Mean Time and the passage of time as well? I don't even have time to read a *Brief History of Time*. Reader's Digest offered classic condensed books for people who shudder at the size of *War and Peace*. Three hundred pages down to six. *Pegs* wouldn't be a good candidate, but *Zen* and *Time*, maybe. YouTube put Readers Digest out of business. Why read six pages when you can watch a two-minute video?

So, thanks to Conrad, there we were in Republic, ahead of schedule, dressed in full riding regalia, looking forward to tee shirts, shorts, and firing up the motel air conditioner. I was worried; will it be one of those AC units that takes twenty minutes to figure out, another twenty to push out slightly cooler air, all the while sounding like a 737 lifting off, forcing you to switch the damn thing off and have a conniption fit?

There's not much going on in the midday heat in downtown Republic on Sunday. Savvy people are at the lake on floaties or sitting in the shade. On August 18th, just Conrad and I parading around the main street in our boots and black riding pants, lugging helmets, looking forlorn. I mentioned the clothes were black, right? Black in the heat makes for hot, sweaty, foolish bikers. Several air-conditioned cars passed. Stares through rolled-up windows. Having fun idiots? What a couple of jackasses! Ever heard of AC?

Desperately we searched for an open, air-conditioned shop. Someone, please take us in! For the love of God, rescue us from this blast furnace! Eureka! One coffee-gift shop was open. We ordered lattes and a History of Republic souvenir book. Kidding! We ordered sodas with extra ice and a Brussels sprout croissant. Kidding again! We ordered eclairs and were way too hot and bothered to thumb a magazine, let alone a turgid history book without a speck of motorcycle news. Sodas done, we took our time inspecting the gift-ware, enjoying the coolness. We examined the porcelain made in China, figurines without making a purchase. Same for the Republic, Washington fridge magnets, with one eye alert for the commissioned salesperson waiting to pounce and give us the hard sell. Prey on our vulnerability. "Your wife would love this one. Don't want to go home empty-handed, do you boys?" *No, we'd rather have cheap figurines thrown at us. Got any expensive jewelry or gardening stuff?*

Here's a note to the shop owner: while it's clever entrepreneurship to diversify in small markets, take advice—dump the marketing consultant's gift-ware idea and add motorcycle accessories. It's rider-country hereabouts, with a popular annual rally site close by. Guaranteed sales when Conrad, I, or the other hundred bikers drop in. Also, tell the *History of Republic* author to include some motorcycle photos! We know Republic enjoys a proud two-wheel history.

Finally, when we could offer no reasonable explanation for our failure to purchase a figurine, we left the sweet coolness, pulled our jackets on, climbed on our GTs, to head west on Highway 20 toward Omak. It was around one-thirty. Conrad had us dawdling, trying not to arrive before check-in time. It's cooler in motion, moving along the highway. We connected by intercom for the occasional chit-chat. A distraction? Yes, but also a way to stay alert and share pertinent information. Is that Dicky hiding up ahead? Take immediate evasive action! "Lock on bearing two niner." Conrad would lapse into military jargon. *What the fuck are you talking about, sailor?*

The bikes cruised along on the outskirts of Republic, doing little more than the posted fifty mile an hour limit, passing large hobby farms and pine forest. Not much traffic in either direction. Great visibility and perfect road conditions. MRR low key, no reason to get the drones circling. Visors open, other than the heat, pretty much ideal. Log another safe riding day. A short day. A bit of a being-stubborn-in-a-good-way day. We'd pass through the Cascade mountains and drop to the Pacific Ocean on Monday. Motorcycling as it should be.

We were in a wildlife area. Folklore has it that dawn and dusk are prime activity hours. Unlike mad dogs and Englishmen, deer know better than to leap about in the midday heat. They have their own set of survival rules. Don't Do Something Stupid, includes lying low in blast furnace weather.

Here's a Best Practice Tip for spotting wildlife:

Think like a hunter.

If you're already a hunter, you're home-free. If not, read hunting tips in Field and Stream, watch Alaska TV survival shows, and sign up for a gun course. In a few years, you'll be ready to resume motorcycling unless you've taken up hunting and have run out of time, in which case read *A Brief History of Time*, smarten up, and get your priorities straight!

Other than Conrad and his wild turkey, we had a clean record. When we leave wildlife alone, we expect the same courtesy in return—a peaceful co-existence. A pact endorsed by PETA without need for UN peacekeepers. Conrad and I are naturally respectful of wildlife, not to the same extent as the Buddha's list, which includes malaria-infected mosquitoes and cockroaches, but then we're jackasses, not gods. Our pets, Pearl and Axel, will verify our good standing, despite the occasional kick in the ribs. Kidding! They never kicked us. They're our ambassadors, spreading the word with their feral friends. We're so proud; here's a photo:

My dog Pearl and Conrad's Axle

Suppose a troublesome renegade beast were to break our agreement. As expert riders on sophisticated machines, we'd call on our skills, execute an instinctual maneuver, and avoid whatever problem arose. All angles were covered, but.

You. Just. Never. Can. Tell.

Take Conrad's turkey on the American prairie. Flat. Open. Uneventful. Not the best place to launch a sneak attack. But the gobbler did. "Maybe it knew about the element of surprise," Marta offered? "Strike when least expected." It was down, flat to the ground on its belly, waiting to spring. Trained by PETA? Beyond Pearl's and Axel's sphere of influence? Or deaf to their declaration: "Let them pass! Our masters respect wild-life! They're anti-animal holocaust, but do enjoy a free-range steak, as do we, now and then."

I had a plan to deal with the worst-case scenarios, should my number come up. A secret weapon, my old desert riding skills. I'd done some dipsy doodling that street riders never get to do. Using my dirt bike experience, I'd put my bike into a slide and walk away with a damaged machine, an insurance claim, and a few minor bruises. Or attack the obstacle like a berm and jump over it. Maybe do a 360 before landing? No need to worry when you've studied motorcycle physics. Especially in the scorching midday heat when animals hunker down under cover, knowing the GT guys respect wildlife.

It didn't happen that way. There's always a smart ass, a renegade. A trouble maker. Flunked out of cubs. Told to hunker down until it cools, they do the opposite.

When your number comes up, kryptonite disarms your secret power, and shit happens. I don't know how it works, it just does, but it's similar to string theory.

A huge horny stag, a bit larger than Blue, Paul Bunyan's legendary ox, hid in the pine forest. He watched the two pretty GT does approach on the road. The first was dark-colored and not his type, but the second was pure white with a super cute sexy teal accent along her flank. Granted, she was moving faster than the stag liked, and she had a weird lump sitting on her back, but she would most definitely do.

The stag was on the high side of the road, in a crouch, hidden by the forest. Paul Bunyan was gone, but Deadeye rested in nonchalant immobility, rifle cocked. The stag calculated speed and distance, ready to spring at precisely the right moment. This doe was his! He had the computation abilities of NASA and impeccable timing, fine-tuned with a power boost of deer testosterone. His judge of distance was bang on, and his landing precise.

In the grip of lust, he failed to hear the forest creatures singing Pearl and Axel's message in gentle harmony, "The word is, these two are alright. Let them pass."

I had no inkling. My radar wasn't focused on impending doom. No notion I was in danger of colliding with a buck suffering from lust and heatstroke. In the moments just before our encounter, I ruminated that Pink Floyd's *Time* would be another excellent song to include in Steve's *Brief History of Time*. Will Conrad make the necessary schedule adjustment so I won't have to convince the motel desk clerk that checking out hours early is a fair trade for checking in minutes early?

Slap–MRR's running fine, everything under control.

I saw a pair of enormous antlers in front of my tiny windscreen. Our eyes locked in a perverted stare for a split second. I was about to be assaulted.

Rule #8, Your Number May Come Up, trumps what little we know about outsmarting destiny. Doesn't matter that you've been diligently on the lookout, following an ex-military scout, have exceptional skills, and a perfect bike; when your number comes up, you're getting a prize, like it or not. Had I been one hundred percent focused on wildlife, I still would not have seen Horace the Horrible lurking, targeting my GT, until it was too late to react. Suicidal stealth deer are impossible to defend against. It's like the earth opening up a smidgeon in front of you. It happens *out of the blue*. I can hear Risk Mitigation Guy triumphantly declaring, "Told you so! Should have bought that tank! Oh, no. Don't listen to a risk expert. What do they know?"

Fuck you, Risk Mitigation Guy! Sit in your god damn tank and gloat. At least skiers are uncaged. I'll take my chances. I'd rather face the consequences than listen to your constant; *the sky is falling rhetoric!*

My stag was more precise than the ten-pound gobbler that launched itself out of a ditch and landed just off target on the right side of Conrad's RT. Had the clandestine animal revenge movement become more sophisticated? Every so often, you hear about slaughter animals escaping on their way to the abattoir, not because Forgetful Pants failed to secure the door—no, it's because animals are waking up and fighting back.

To them, we're Nazis. Who can blame them? We've forced wildlife to declare war on us. Political scientists, stop flipping dead meat and get on this!

Horace the Horrible

Back to Horace... in an instant, his enormous rack of antlers appeared in front of my mini windscreen. It wasn't Christmas eve; unless Rudolph and Santa were conducting summer training runs in the area, I knew I was in serious trouble. I saw antlers. Did I tell you they were enormous? As the expression goes, there was *fuck all I could do about it*. Sighting through his high-tech laser scope, DD pulled the trigger. Duck going down! GT knocked to shit. Driver, claim your lotto prize. Death Lottery winner as well?

Bang on target was precisely right. He was on target, and we went BANG! I heard the impact; it was deafening even with earplugs and wearing a helmet, blasting over the wind and engine noise. That in-the-moment-crushing impact sound can't be described. Yes, it's deafening and terrifying, but it also carries the sound of tragedy, like the scream of a bunny being skinned alive. The other Steve, Mr. King, probably nailed it in one of his horror stories. The sound of my motorcycle colliding with Horace was otherworldly, and that's Mr. King's forte.

I went up and came down. That was it; in the end, there wasn't much to tell. Like Mary's accident, summarized in her medical notes as: "She flew over the handlebars and hit her bare head on the pavement when she landed." The rest of the notes are fluff. If they made a Reader's Digest condensed novella about my crash, it would say, "He went up and came down." End of story.

The microsecond before contact, I realized what was about to happen— like a sped-up version of standing on a ship deck, in shark-infested waters, watching torpedoes lock-in. Or being in the Secret Bunker witnessing impending nuclear annihilation on the radar screen. I didn't engage the brake, move to turn the bike, or go into a defensive slide. The expert dipsy doodling maneuvers I carried in my head, the insurance I possessed that would get me out of trouble if I had to avoid an obstacle quickly, failed to translate to physical action. You can only do so much in an unexpected half-second—no time to save yourself.

Truth About Motorcycling: you can become
as helpless as a newborn baby.

At sixty miles an hour, I rode straight into a three-hundred-pound barrier, putting myself at the mercy of physics, luck, traffic, my riding gear, and my physical capability to withstand Newton's laws of force, the impending collision with the ground. No choice but to be a Guinea pig. Just like Mary, except she had done something stupid, and I had not.

I wonder what the Buddha, resting in the circuitry, thought when we crashed? Must have scared the shit out of Him. Did my crash cause his Holiness to think differently about universal truths? Or was Robert Pirsig whistling Dixie? I'm not sure. Or perhaps Buddha wandered into the bush to console Horace during his passage through the Valley of Death? He'd do it for a snake in the grass, so why not a sex-crazed stag?

Rule #8, restated with a more fatalistic bent, says:

There are only two kinds of bikers: those that have been down and those that are going to go down.

It's a blessing that there is no time to think when something potentially deadly happens. No moments of panic. No terror. No, *please God, I promise to do better if you rescue me from this unforeseen, shitty, horrific development. You do validate don't You, forgive all sins?* No second-guessing your decision to ride a few more years before hanging up the keys with an unblemished record. Rent a tank RV and visit the Secret Bunker in Scotland.

When you come to an unexpected, instantaneous stop on a motorcycle, bad things happen. Your limbs get caught and snap as you rocket off the bike. Your head hasn't even touched down, and you're already fucked-up. Too late to review your protective gear choices. No checking to see if you forgot to fasten your helmet strap correctly or if your boots are snapped tight.

VALLEY OF DEATH

Horace and I have collided, but I haven't hit the ground yet. While I'm still flying, like a circus clown shot from a cannon without a net to land in, I should tell you another near-death story.

I almost drowned, in a river, like Bob. A friend and I were in a canoe until it capsized. Then we were in the ice melt, spring run-water of a major river. Drowning takes time; it's nothing like being shot off a motorcycle. They say your life flashes before you when your mind realizes death is imminent—it happened to me. I was ready to let go. Stop struggling. Slip under the water. Float into the Valley of Death. But fate intervened and dragged me out, minutes before I was to become fish food.

I wonder if Bob got a video? And if he did, was I in it?

I didn't get a replay of the life-flashing-before-my-eyes video when I was flying through the air, nor as I lay on Highway 20. True, I had already seen it once, but there'd been years of living added since my first close call. Not even a clip of the new material played. Maybe there's a time calculation involved? Vehicle accident, no video due to lack of time. Slow, like dying of cancer or starvation. No video because you have plenty of time for self-review. Drowning is in the sweet spot.

More important than time, in all cases, there can be no doubt the subject is about to enter the Valley of Death. When I almost drowned, I was certain. It wasn't "I'm scared to death" or "in a life and death struggle." *Yea, though I walk through the Valley of the Shadow of Death; I will fear no Evil.* That's how it was for me in the fast-flowing river, with hypothermia and a belly full of water. I was at peace, done, ready to let go and pass through the Valley of Death. Into the arms of God and Motorcycle Heaven. It's the only supernatural experience I've had. *Fear no evil.* It's a good one to carry in your back pocket in case you collide with a large animal. The Valley of Death had a profound effect on my development; without it, I'd be a Total Asshole instead of simply just another Jackass. Or perhaps a Political Scientist or Blockhead?

I'm now on the descent leg of the parabolic arc of my post-Horace-encounter, pre-hit-the-road flight. I'm propelled toward the ground like a North Korean test missile. Peace and harmony are not considerations. I'm a renegade projectile at war with the world, with my head perfectly positioned to be the first point of contact. The evidence suggests the reality of what happened—first my helmet, and then my shoulder took the initial blow. Then, my hip smashed into the ground. I might have bounced, a raggedy-bone doll skimming like a rock over the pavement.

Flesh and blood versus asphalt. It's not a fair fight. Not a thing you can do about it. You can be stubborn in a good way, but what's the point? You've won the lottery:

The Jig's Up, You Move from Motorcycle Riding Rules to God's Rules.

FEAR NO EVIL

I t all happened in the time it takes to change the TV channel. Mortals cannot comprehend the reality of the journey of human tumbleweed. Flying blind, lost in the Secret Bunker of my mind, not focused on the inescapable big bang ahead of me. The great news is you're just there, in the moment, already with broken bones, not worried about the stopping part because you're numb. No need to question: will I live or die? Or walk again? Drool like a bloodhound waiting for food? There are no thoughts of how dressing in haute couture will work with those bags you have to pee into. You won't even have time to think about how you'll never have to worry about shitting your pants again—because your plumbing's out of order. Covered with cobwebs.

So, if you're ever in this unfortunate situation, here's the best tip I've got:

Enjoy your time in the air. It's not going to get better.

Afterward, when the flight is over and the capsule has crash-landed, these words will scream inside your head: *this is about to hurt like hell, isn't it?* Take a brief inventory of body parts, and you'll be thinking, *nope, not like hell, it's* way *worse,* if you're still thinking.

In Bill Bryson's book *Down Under* he recounts the

story of a man stung by a box jellyfish widely thought of as having the most painful sting of all forms of wildlife. In his story, when the man is stung, he begins to scream louder than virtually any person in history. Paramedics come and sedate him and take him off to the hospital. Here's the kicker: even sedated. He was still screaming.

So maybe the next tip should be:

> *If you're lying on the road screaming, think of that guy on an Aussie beach and count your lucky stars that box jellyfish prefer water.*

Bill's Nameless Screamer probably never rode a motorcycle, so naturally, he was upset. If you're fired off a bike thanks to wildlife, you'll think, *at least I got a ride in beforehand.* Poor Screamer was wading in shallow water, killing time, when Mother Nature attacked him. No wonder he screamed blue murder. No motorcycle preJOY!

Presently, I'm lying face up in the middle of the road, the hot orange-yellow August sun frying me like meat under the broiler at Tony's deli. Like being on an Aussie beach, a relentless sun, except bordered by a green pine forest instead of blue waves and jellyfish. A beautiful day for Horace the Horrible to die a miserable death. I have no recollection of bones snapping, of going over the bars and sailing through the air before the asphalt, ever so efficiently, stopped my fall and my tissues, organs, bones and muscles absorbed the impact energy.

My mind ducked down and covered itself with a

warm baby blanket. You'd think it would be in a frenzy, filing reports, testing limbs, and having a serious conversation with God, but it didn't have a clue; it was empty, like a political scientist looking at a math test.

Left Brain and Right Brain were chatting:

"Duck and cover, under that blanket."

"Save ourselves," said Left.

Brain Brian (right), ever the child followed readily, agreeing, "There's nothing we can do! We'll check in later if we're still ticking." Right peeked out from under the mental safety blanket and saw both bike and body wrecked. Conrad was swinging his machine around, horrified. "We're deep in the brown smelly stuff, that's for sure."

With that, my mind shut down as MRR reached over and tapped *Fear No Evil* in my back pocket. *You take it from here, Fear. Who knows if I'll be back? Doesn't look good.*

No part of my body tried to move; I felt no urgency to do anything other than lie back and accept the consequences of my motorcycle choice. If the friends of Horace had dispatched an army of spiders, snakes, and jellyfish on a revenge mission, I wouldn't have cared. How much worse can it get?

At some point, my brain popped up again, on minimal cycles. Slowly, like an old computer running a glitchy operating system, it wondered about the body, the way one thinks about the outcome of a football game. As Captain, I needed a damage assessment:

Seal off bulkhead compartment three!

It's beyond hope, Captain!

We're going down if it can't be repaired!

Nerves reported back. Our ship's not intact Captain. We may go down. Unorthodox body behaviors were observed, but no white-hot daggers like Lenny described. Sometimes it's best to leave well enough alone and not go looking for trouble. Allow your mind to cower under the blanket. *What can I do? Bulkhead compartment three will have to seal itself. I'm not afraid to walk in the Valley of Death. Lying on the pavement in the scorching sun isn't as peaceful as drowning in a river, but it's not that bad. At least it's warm.*

Brain Brian looked at its cards, thought *Left can handle this*, and out of respect for the little it knew about survival, elected to fold. Unable to cope in a situation too esoteric for most, the overwhelmed grey matter threw in its hand and yelled, "Pass," leaving Left alone to run the ship. Thanks to Left, I remained calm. No hysterics or sense of urgency. *Just lie here like a deflated blow-up doll and wait.*

"No sense getting bent out of shape," Left said calmly, with a light chuckle at the irony. "A semi may run us over, but, hey ho, that's life and death for us at this point. At least we died tryin'."

Doctors say there is a release of endorphins and adrenaline to increase physical alertness and elevate mood, making it easier to handle a crash. The hormones block pain and stress to keep you calm. I must have had a ton of anti-anxiety hormones circulating, enough to allow me to relax in the middle of the highway, in the scorching heat, content to let fate unfold. There was an acceptance, like drowning in the river, except I expected I'd soon be up duct taping GT back together.

The pain wasn't like a Charlie-horse, sudden and severe. It seeped slowly into my nothingness. "Remain perfectly still, and the pain will fade," Brain ordered. "Rest awhile, and then we'll try organizing our parts. Maybe try to stand up."

Moving would surely please Conrad, who now stood over me, looking distressed and probably thinking: *Will I have to spoon-feed him soup when I visit from now on? Shove those soft jelly candies he detests through his dribbling gums? Maybe sneak in a Brussels sprout as a joke? Ha ha, that would be funny. Bet he'll make the most disgusting gurgling noises when we go out for coffee. How long till I can stop dropping by?* These are obvious thoughts when you come across a person jettisoned off of a motorcycle, and that person is your friend.

In my shock-induced trance, I stood unaided, and imagined strangers circled me, applauding, "He's up, with all that gear on. Dodged a bullet! What a great attitude! Look at the size of those boots! Could have been worse, that's for sure." And I'd say to Conrad, *Everything's all right, buddy. Just a bump—give me a moment or two to compose myself, and we'll be on our way. You can MacGyver GT together, right? You're good at sorting things out."*

But all I could do was lie in a calm daze, Fearing No Evil. I couldn't speak. Conrad spoke, but I couldn't make out what he was saying. *What's that you say, Conrad?* I asked (if 'asking' really means 'staring blankly'). Conrad repeated his question, given my lack of response—could I move off the center line toward the side of the road? I almost died laughing (if 'laughing' really means 'staring blankly').

Sensible idea though, Left said after analyzing the situation. *Not getting run over is a sound course of action. Let's work on it, work it... Get our parts moving.* The left side of my body, from the shoulder down, was inoperable, dead weight. Broken, fractured, inflamed, bruised, and leaking. The absence of massive mind-numbing pain signals meant my body would be responsive soon, I thought. My right leg pushed me over an inch. Couldn't manage more. "That inch will have to do," Left muttered. "All we got, I'm afraid."

Thankfully, vehicles had stopped, and the road was soon blocked, so not even that inch was necessary. Bystanders were horrified (except a delighted, show-me-the-blood type, lad). Lying flat on my back, like a corpse, it was impossible to observe what was going on, but I was vaguely aware of commotion as I reinforced the foolishness of motorcycle riding. One of the congregated turned out to be an Emergency Medical Technician, and another was a nurse. How lucky is that? What are those odds? My number came up, but part of the prize was angels of mercy.

The EMT took charge. I didn't have to do a thing; I was in the hands of Super Samaritan. He issued instructions, established control. Impressed the hell out of Left Brain. He also positioned two ladies in front to act as a sunscreen. What a guy; what an outstanding job! I looked at the two new arrivals, unable to say *thank you, ladies. I'm sure this isn't what you had planned for your Sunday afternoon outing. Stopping in this blazing heat for sun blocker duty?* They smiled down at me, without complaint, and did an outstanding job–both were stout, robust women: I suppose that's why Super Samaritan selected them. One reminded me of my Auntie Minnie.

"Do not move your head!" *Okay, I'm fine with that. I won't argue about whether I have the right to do whatever I choose to do with my head. Not the best time to drag out my debating skills.* Better to remain a pleasant, cooperative blob. Super Samaritan performed medical checks. Questions were asked. In good hands, I was told. "Lie still. Do not move! Remain conscious and wait for the ambulance to arrive. Who's the dumbass now? Like I was going anywhere soon. *Okay, no problem.* I used facial expressions to pass information along and uttered childlike sounds. *No need to make a fuss. Give me a minute. I'll get up and be on my way soon. You're all excellent people, but it's too much. Unnecessary. Really. Just give me a few minutes. Wait... Did you say ambulance?*

I didn't recall ordering an ambulance.

"You'll be all right. I'm going to dribble some water into your mouth now." Super Samaritan assured me. "Relax." I did a good job relaxing and even managed a few swallows of the cool liquid with my helmet on and visor up. Half of it ran down my chin. Let the drooling commence! *Yes, I know I'll be all right,* I wanted to answer; *after all, I almost drowned once. I understand what it's like to drift toward the Valley of Death. This isn't it. I'm fine. Let me sleep. Thanks for your concern. You're incredibly nice, folks, and damn fine sun blockers!*

People carried on one-sided conversations with me to keep me alert. I wondered if the good Samaritans appreciated my *Fear No Evil* demeanor? No hollering blue murder and carrying on like the Screamer with the teeny weenie jellyfish sting. Australians can be so over-the-top.

 A state trooper attended the accident scene. I saw his enormous hat pointed down at me. It did a good job blocking the sun from his face, like the two ladies standing over me. Conrad told him about the deer. The cop seemed suspicious; *it's always a deer.* Never, *truth be told, he was behaving like a Blockhead, officer.* "Don't worry about your bike," Conrad told me. He would collect what I needed, especially the emergency travel insurance document in the top box. He'd look after GT. So, they wandered off to inspect the evidence.

Lots of sirens. Each one with a unique sound. The state trooper's first. Then a fire truck, followed shortly by the ambulance. It wasn't low-key. A real hullaballoo. Motorcycle accident! One victim. Logged into the system. Full response code red! Sirens wailing. Lights flashing. Hospital Emergency ready for incoming. Futile to resist. No chance of doing a low-key duct tape, zap strap, repair and carry-on job now. "You'll be all right," Super Samaritan kept reminding me. It was unnerving. *Why would I not be alright?*

From the recently arrived ambulance came an on-duty EMT who carefully replaced my helmet with a neck brace. My head was locked in, unable to move. My riding pants had zippers up the legs — my pants came off. The EMT explained that they cut most riding pants off. I smiled. Yes, my lucky day! I'll be needing those pants to ride home soon.

In a professional drill that involved counting, they hoisted my body up and onto a stretcher. I was very impressed. First-class, not like some hunter found me and dragged my ass into the back of their old pickup beside a moose carcass.

They placed me in the ambulance, covered with a thin blanket, hooked up to an IV drip, and gave me some pills. No one asked if I  wanted a ride. When you're in an accident, things happen to you; you don't have a say. You're like beef on route to a processing plant, except with the opposite intent. The siren wailed, and off we went, headed east, back the way we came, toward the coffee-gift shop— my first ambulance ride. GT was abandoned, crippled, and alone. *Poor thing.*

It had been quiet, peaceful, and serene in the river.

It's a nice way to go, drowning. No one fussed over me, into the world alone, out of the world alone. Not at all like having a motorcycle accident on an American highway. It's was a great big hullaballoo.

It's impressive how organized rescue and repair processes snatch and take them in for repair. Their routines are devoid of indecision. If you're the body, you'll be part of a military-like operation staffed by friendly angels of mercy. I wonder if they ever get pissed off? Have bad days? Thanks a lot, asshole! I was in the middle of binging Breaking Bad and eating nachos. Not in a mood to be comforting, but you'll still be getting our HUMONGOUS BILL!

Left whispered, "What's that? A big bill?"

"I'll have to pay for all this?"

"We're not in the land of socialized medicine; they don't roll fire trucks for free here."

"I'll be charged for the fire truck? Nothing's on fire! I'll be charged even though I didn't place an order?"

"Yup, you will" Left said. Matter-of-factly. "Costs are heading toward the stratosphere, and we have no say. Too bad you didn't read your el cheapo insurance policy."

Brain Brian popped up from nowhere and rattled on hysterically, repeating the financial-medical horror stories we had taken in over the years. I visualized the billing meter going round and round, like carnival ducks, picking up speed with every revolution and siren blare.

I don't know if it was the financial scare, the pain, or the drugs, but I passed out.

PART 6: WELCOME TO BLOBLAND

FERRY MEMORIAL

Hospitals around the globe are at the forefront of the motorcyclist repair business. Can't be repaired? Of course, they also have morgues —though there's less money in dead people. And less looking after—unless you call adjusting the freezer temperature good hospitality.

Ferry County Memorial Hospital in Republic Washington, established in 1945, is surrounded by great motorcycle roads and staffed by angels of mercy. The hospital doesn't promote the motorcycle roads despite the significant revenue  that flows into their coffers from the rivers of damaged bikers that stream through its doors. Ferry Memorial mainly attends to clueless weekend warriors and SQUIDS. Don't you know what a SQUID is? It's a case of you know-one-when-you-see-one. Nonetheless, I turned to the Urban Dictionary to get you a better definition:

> A young motorcyclist who overestimates his abilities boasts of his riding skills when in reality he has none. SQUID bikes are usually decorated with chrome and various anodized bits. Rear tires are

too wide for their own good, swingarm extended. Really slow in the corners, and sudden bursts of acceleration when a straight appears. SQUIDs wear no protection, deeming themselves invincible. This fact compounds itself with the fact that they engage in 'extreme riding,' performing wheelies and stoppies in public areas. SQUIDs wreck a lot. A contraction of the phrase **'squirrely kid'**.

It isn't easy, though, even for experienced hospital staff to tell Blockheads from SQUIDs from the seasoned experts—they all look alike on stretchers, pantless, wearing neck braces. They're all incoming from the "impact injury generators."

Everyone likes to put their best foot forward. Make a good impression. How did they size me up the day they wheeled me in? I'll never know, but I'll always wonder. They process many downed ducks because I kept hearing, "You're not our first one..." It's a stock phrase repeated to make the incoming feel better. Thank God, I thought! *They're experienced. They know how to repair crash victims. It's OK that I'm pant-less and vulnerable, like when I was two years old. Biker Lives Matter at Ferry Memorial.*

Tough guy and gal bikers aren't so carefree and bold when they're wounded and scared half to death. Their joyous, the world is my oyster, outlaw ride of Zen self-discovery, brought to a crashing halt by an attempt to be one with the Earth. I was in the group that avoided the black guideline on the hospital floor — "Follow Black to the Morgue"—and then, "Welcome to Our Morgue," instead I rode the red line to the ER. *Is that a painted line, or is it my blood trail dripping off the gurney?* The ride to ER is shorter than the morgue trip, which is downstairs, at the end of the hall, next to the boiler room. ER is always beside Admin, where they prepare your massive bill.

Riders never foresee their adventures ending in the ER. Despite this certainty it's always a shock:

It's a matter of when, not if.

Riders take confidence in their Cone School diploma, track or dirt ribbons, Iron Butt credentials, or the power of their gang, but it all counts for diddly squat on an Emergency Room gurney. "Thought it would never happen to me," their terrified expressions tell the angels of mercy. The nurses know better. "Believe me, honey... you're not the first one who thought that. Yet, here you are. Strange how that works, huh? So predictable." They frown at Risk Management Guy—he's a business killer. *Get the fuck outta here, asshole!*

Hospitals are intimidating when you're not familiar with their mysterious ways and are lying in a supine position, without pants, in a head restraint, pumped full of drugs, which are needed because the emergency examination beds are about as comfortable as hot highway pavement. The nurses were friendly as they performed the requisite medical checks—it was like having my mom, aunts, and sisters there just before kindergarten nap time. The left side of my brain hadn't yet come up with a plan beyond, *wait it out. Soon they'll be done. One step at a time. Slap on a couple of Band-Aids. Eventually, they'll let us move, swivel Head around, and rise from the examination table like the second coming of Christ (maybe a tad overstated, more like - move Head thirty degrees to each side and creak forward while holding flimsy hospital dress down). Conrad will sort things out and we'll be on our way.*

A giant needle appeared, wheeled in by a smiling, gentle-faced nurse. I hate needles. When I was young, I struggled to remain upright at the sight of a needle or a drop of blood. Age has hardened me; now, I merely tremble. Needle Nurse had turned into the psycho who tortures an author in Steven King's *Misery. Kathy Bates is working at Ferry Memorial?* Now, I was shaking. "Just an Aspirin, please, and I'll be on my way," Left suggested.

"When you come out of shock, you'll need it," the Needle Nurse told me, waving her massive spike. "You're not my first. Believe me." I didn't believe her and almost asked to see her qualifications before she could skewer me. *Are you certified to use that thing? Did you attend Humongous Needles, a Gentler Approach, last month? Or you're old school? Step forward. Thrust. Reload.*

Then I asked myself, who am I, a former fainter, to question medical experts? *They know the drill. It's not new to them. Would I tell Valentino Rossi how to take a corner? No! Question Professor Hawking's decisions if we were floating around the Cosmos together? No! No! Second guess my motorcycle mechanic with his "Secret Spe-*

cialty Tool Certification" diploma? *No!*

I could imagine what the rescuers would think: *Listen to this impact injury, biker-idiot! Why do we bother? After all, we've done for him, sirens, first ride in an ambulance, saving his life, not cutting his pants, even sent the fire truck, he's asking to see our certificates? How dare he? I'm not just going to jab him; I'm going to stab him. May use the unnecessarily larger needle. Shut the fuck up! Asshole! Why are you trembling?*

The thought of upsetting Needle Nurse scared me even more than her giant needle. Experience taught me—you must not offend your bike mechanic. It's inappropriate to question the authorities, especially local by-law officers and motel front desk staff. I didn't want to come across as a hospital SQUID. I accepted the stabbing, and in truth, I'm glad I did. Seems Needle Nurse knew her stuff and did one hell of a job. Drugs have a way of changing your perspective, and hospitals have beautiful medicines. The best ones come in huge needles.

Time passed; the doctor, "Is on his way." The nursing staff didn't allow movement. Luckily, I had stopped trembling. I was stiff as a board and concerned the doc would be less than pleased about being called out on a Sunday to repair another selfish joyrider. *Do you outlaws have absolutely no consideration for others? Good business, but doctors need days off too, you know?*

One of the nurses was from BC. She has relatives in Victoria, which made us practically family. Married an American, and the couple visits Vancouver Island frequently. It's weird: if you're damaged or in dire straits and away from home, meeting a person from your neck of the woods cements a bond. Based purely on geography, a total stranger will bend over backward to help you. Location supercharges an inherent natural desire to assist. BC Nurse looked at me; I'm here for you. With Conrad, we were geographically bonded, a Holy Trinity.

Is there a hospital version of dash-and-dine, I wondered? I couldn't rely on Gigantic Insurance Company to spring me. Everyone's heard insurance horror stories; desperate policy holders abandoned in their hour of need. I had zero experience dealing with insurers, other than one minor fender bender. I'd heard plenty of *the devil is an insurance adjuster* stories, though. They're way more badass than motorcycle outlaws.

Once the doc looks me over, I'll be declared fit as a fiddle, I deluded myself. A well-used fiddle, for sure, and somewhat knocked around, out of tune, and scraped up but capable of making music. Good enough to satisfy Ferry Memorial's obligations. *He can play Twinkle Twinkle. OK, good to go. We can't hold him any longer.*

I debated, is the Motorcycle Injury Phone Call necessary? Needlessly worry family? Send them off in a tizzy. Am I capable of secretly sorting this out? After all, I put myself in Ferry Memorial; shouldn't I get myself out? It's not like anyone forced me to ride motorcycles. Buckle down and take care of business. No foofaraw! Soreness passes with time. Conrad knows how to sort things out. Make use of his military training.

Flee the battle zone!

The emergency doctor, a young man, arrived for the examination. Left and Right muttered quietly, impressed and a little intimidated. At his side, an x-ray technician waited his turn; the tech mentioned that he had been called in on his day off, though he didn't seem upset about it: "Not the first time." he said. I wondered if he did piece work? Per motorcyclist? Is that the way private medicine works?

I mentally uttered some coherent words in response to the doctor's questions and told him my version. "It was a close call. I'm battered but intact and ready to climb on and ride away. Duct tape me up, throw on one of those white cloth bandage wraps, perhaps one around my head for dramatic effect. A little more rest, and I'm good to go. Could you spare a few zap straps for GT? I'll pay for them, of course. Add them to my bill. I'm sure Gigantic Insurance Company won't notice." Truthfully, though, all I said was, "Hi, Doc." Even that was more grunt than discernible. I wondered, what's the price of a hospital a tie strap?

"Hi, back at ya," he replied. "I see you've had quite the accident. Totaled your motorbike? I hear you killed Blue? You're not the first impact injury we've seen here, but I can't remember anyone killing Blue before."

Hospital humor? Too far west for Paul Bunyan's big ox. "Stag," I whispered. "Quite a bit larger than Blue." I thought about playing along with the humor. *Did anyone see Buddha wandering around the forest? He's a hefty fellow—easy to spot. He wasn't injured, was he?* But what if one of the staff is a devout Buddhist? Or respectful of all religions? Don't turn a nurse into *Misery's* Kathy Bates. Such a godless heathen! Strap him to the slab! Follow the black line to the boiler room. He'll be ready for a freezer drawer soon.

No one would get my joke. Not even BC Nurse. It'd fall flat on the emergency room floor. Dead. Only Marta would get it, and she wasn't at Ferry Memorial. So, I'd try to explain, give up, and shrug, "Read *Zen and the Art of Motorcycle Maintenance*."

"Yes, very sad indeed," the doctor said, mishearing.

"Stag!" I croaked again.

"Yes, it was sad." Now he was looking at me like I was a repetitive idiot. So, I gave up.

A few preliminaries later, the physical exam began.

"Wiggle your toes, please," instructed the doc.

Do you start with Toes because they are furthest from Head? A medical diagnostic hard rule? I was super confident I could put my toes up against any toes in Emergency on that Sunday afternoon.

I passed Toes with flying colors, aced it, as they say.

"Finger movement?"

I wasn't as finger confident. My left shoulder was locked, but I could force my elbow to bend slightly. So, I twitched my left fingers and finished with a flourish of movement using my right hand.

Good enough? I wanted to put on a show for the nice doctor. *At least there's movement. Not like Toes, but Fin-*

gers work. I'm no doctor, but even I can see, they just need rest.

My eyes followed his finger as requested. At least I thought so. It's much harder to tell with Eyes than with Toes or Fingers. I didn't have a clue, and the doctor wasn't about to provide an opinion. The legalities of the trade and American litigation kept him zipped up. He nodded occasionally and didn't act horrified, both excellent signs. *See? All this is unnecessary. I should clear out, make way for a needy impact injury patient. I'm sure a SQUID will be along shortly.*

Then the big test. Carefully, my neck brace came off. The doctor's fingers poked around the base of my skull. I could move Head on command. *Hallelujah! Toes, Fingers, Eyes, and now Head. All is well! Let's wrap this up.*

"OK?" I asked. "I can go?"

The doctor wore his not-so-fast-buster expression and spoke using language he thought I would probably understand, "Just because the wheels turn on a motorcycle doesn't mean to say it's drivable. At Ferry, we need to check you're OK, so diagnostic investigations are mandatory. I'm your mechanic, so to speak. Robert," he said, gesticulating to the X-Ray technician, "Will make sure none of your forks are broken, and check for hairline cracks in your frame." That's what I heard as the doc rolled out his medical school terminology. I didn't catch any terrifying words like, "paralyzed," "spine," or "Mary McGregor," so I relaxed. More waiting. Just like at Service. It's always takes longer than you think.

Robert grabbed the end of the gurney, and we headed off to take pictures, following the blue line. More than a dozen shots up and down my left side. "We'll do a CAT scan on Monday," the technician said, "You're not the first one we've had, so we know to look for bleeds on the brain and other stuff you wouldn't understand. Doctor's orders. You'll be transferred to regional for an MRI."

I wasn't listening. I waited, biding my time because that's what you do in Service. Keep your mouth shut and wait. No toe X-rays, I wanted to ask? *They were also in the accident. Yes, I was wearing my big boots but also a helmet, and you want to check my brain? Seems a bit selective, don't you think? More money in brains than toes? Any idea what a hospital zap strap is worth? I'll need a few to get GT back on the road.*

Robert mentioned the word "MRI," again. And "ambulance ride Monday to the regional hospital." Not that I won't enjoy another ambulance ride on drugs, but the medical process was spinning out of control and becoming ridiculous. Billing horror stories cut through the drug fog. *It's all true, and it's happening to me! This is precisely how they do it. With drugs and regional hospitals. I need an escape plan!* I hadn't lost an arm and a leg in the accident, but I was about to lose my shirt. I imagined a colossal dollar meter by the door relentlessly ticking up my bill. And what about poor GT? Waiting for me. Alone and forsaken in a strange yard, wondering, have I been abandoned? Waiting for me to show up and nurse her home. Away from the scrap yard. Perform reconstructive surgery.

After all, we've been through together. GT never let me down. Not once.

We headed back to the ER. "I'm not allowed to interpret them," Robert said when asked about the results. *Fine, I can wait. Medical boundaries and safeguards are important. Division of duties. I understand.* Unless you ride? One biker to another, right?

MOTORCYCLE HOSPITAL CALL

I rested in a dimly lit room; my left leg raised on a pad, my joints on ice, my mind in Blobland. Conrad was off scouting transportation and accommodation options. "Undrivable," he'd reported back on GT's condition. Nurses dropped in to check on their impact injury. Yes, I'm still here, on ice. It's very reassuring knowing angels are outside the door, not hovering above the bed, waiting to give the Valley of Death tour.

"The doctor will return soon."

BC Nurse located my phone, intact and operational. She slid a second pillow under right shoulder. I picked up my left arm (which had become incapable of movement) with my right hand and swung it over to the phone lying on my chest. Left fingers gripped in the ready-for-action position. *Now what?* Reluctantly, I'd accepted the fact, I must make the call. I would not arrive home on schedule and would have apparent damage when I did. *What have you been up to? Ever heard of communication? The thing that rings?*

But what to say? "Hey, my number finally came up! But splendid news! Hardly a scratch!" I felt guilty. Like an alcoholic who falls off the wagon and calls home, "I'm drunk and disgusting. Come and bail me out."

You did it to yourself, buster! What the hell is wrong with you?

Do riders think only of themselves when they climb on? Gambling, forcing others to deal with the consequences? *No one forced you to buy motorcycles!*

Truth About Motorcycles: motorcycles are like slot machines.

A motorcycle is like buying a time bomb with a live random counter. Families accept the truth about motorcycles; riders chose to ignore it. They haul out the tired phrase: "it's not motorcycles, it's the idiots behind car wheels. I'll be fine." Most riders think they're too aware and agile to have an accident. Not families, they know better.

I rode for years without making the Hospital Call. Not even the Slightly Bruised or Having Mechanical Issues call. It seemed like I might get away Scot-free. It's not impossible.

I rehearsed: be released soon. Just waiting for the doc. Yes, a day or two late. Rule #8, but a fortunate break. I'm right as rain. Fit as a fiddle. You know me, one of the lucky ones.

There is no gentle way to begin a conversation with "hospital" and "motorcycle." My wife is emotional, not a stone-cold semi-Newtonian, like me. Accident conversations are simple between left brains. "Not surprised. It was just a matter of time after you bought that thing. Inevitable. What else is new? Anything unusual or out of the norm?"

I decided to text my daughter, a young nurse, a medical professional. The word "hospital" would not freak her out; she worked at one. We text regularly; nothing unusual about receiving a message from dad. "You there?"

She was. I used the words: hospital, deer, and motorcycle. Most importantly, "I'm fine" and "Conrad." Monica used "OMG" repeatedly. I suggested she break the news to Mom, on account of her freaking out. I would standby to phone once I got the thumbs up. Monica didn't fall for my ploy. "No way. You need to talk to her yourself. Kids are so much easier when they're young and you're godlike.

It went better than expected. Conditioned by years of waiting for the Hospital Call and, "I'm fine. Yes, I'm in a hospital, but it's not a big deal—a formality. You know how these things work. A scratch in a road accident, and they haul your ass to the hospital. Can't be avoided. I'll be out soon. Yes, I bought travel insurance. Yes, Conrad is here. Other than our schedule getting screwed up, everything's hunky-dory. Right as rain. Couldn't be better. Fit as a fiddle."

We didn't get into insurance details, no revealing my worries about opting for the *el cheapo* option. It was immaterial, given I was OK and would be released before long. It was a colossal relief, ticking the call off my to-do list. Next, escape and rescue GT. Haul her home in a rental truck.

I have two sisters and three brothers. I'm the youngest—the baby. I'm used to being coddled. We have a messaging group, Sibs Gang. I snapped a picture of my toes poking out from under the hospital sheet. "Guess where I am?" So that kicked off a flurry of activity. Poor baby! Everyone on standby! Battle stations! Lower the life raft! It's great having two bonus moms and three older brother-protectors.

I also sent the toe picture to the Copley Park Dog Moms. I'm a proud Honorary Dog Mom, thanks to Pearl. That triggered another burst of empathy. Ladies with dogs know how to lay it on thick. I felt the opposite of forsaken.

A nurse switched the lights to stark-sterile-hospital-glare mode. "Doctor is on his way." The ice packs removed; they prepped me to make my second significant medical move of the day. The first being Highway 20-to-gurney-to-hospital examination slab. Other than being there, well... I was just there. But move two would be all me. BC Nurse was my instructor for my bed-to-wheelchair attempt. Very promising, I thought. No bad news, and it's common knowledge, hospitals always show patients the exit door in wheelchairs. No walking out. If you're alive, wheelchair. Deceased, gurney — follow the black line and make a right when you see "Welcome to Our Morgue."

My move was Pivot Transfer, Unassisted in the Standing Position. Looked easy. Stand on operational right leg, supporting myself from the edge of the bed if necessary, pivot, and lower into the locked wheelchair. Rear-end touchdown  must be precise. Don't overshoot! Always double-check to ensure the wheelchair is locked. As a precaution, an orderly held my chair. *I ride a motorcycle, remember? Let's get on with it! A wheelchair is child's play.* I waited patiently, sitting on the edge of the bed in my hospital gown. *The door is just down the corridor. Don't blow this now with inappropriate remarks! This is the last mandatory step before freedom.*

"Absolutely no weight on your left leg!"

I'm a former three-legged race winner. Grade five, I think it was? The moment weight transferred to my right leg, and I pushed off the bed, a rush of pain, from somewhere deep inside my body, yelled, what the fuck do you think you're doing? Don't do that! Get back on the slab-bed and lie perfectly still! Maybe take another round from Needle Nurse. A vile, bitter cocktail rose up my throat.

I waited, holding on to the bed, trying not to reveal distress.

"Take your time."

I straightened up and waited. I hadn't been fully upright since leaving the café. Back when I took standing for granted.

*Truth About Motorcycles: never
take riding for granted.*

Bent at the knee, my left leg was slightly off the ground, which pleased BC Nurse and delighted me.

"Pivot and lower yourself into the chair." Rescuers stood by, ready to grab my fucked-up body if it failed me.

Not smooth, but a success! Pivot transfer sounds trivial, but it's like learning to run the 100-meter hurdles if you're banged up.

 The doctor returned. He held a hospital clipboard, which was new. Out of a meeting with Finance and Administration? I didn't like the look. The clipboard made my guy look less like a TV doctor and more like the service advisor at the local dealership. "Bad news about your bike." They always look down at their clipboard if it's terrible news. You brought it in to have the secret software tweak done, but it's "bad news," and the proof is on the clipboard.

Doc looked at the paperwork and back at me. Come on. Out with it, I wanted to say. You found nothing. Fit as a fiddle. Time to end the foofaraw. *Did they tell you, doc? I nailed pivot transfer.*

He adjusted his glasses and looked down at the

notes to double-check he wasn't handed the medical records for Testicular Cancer Patient #1, then said, "Most motorcycle accidents don't end well. Particularly not when Blue is involved."

So far, so good. Like service adviser saying, "Just had to turn that little impossible to reach adjuster screw with our very expensive secret tool."

"But." He was looking at the clipboard again. "Your left leg is badly broken. We'll schedule surgery. Time is critical."

I felt like he'd punched me in the gut. How can this be? They want to slice me? Shouldn't I be bellowing like an Australian? Never having broken a body part, I had no basis for comparison. I sprained a finger once —hurt a hell of a lot more. *Maybe it's that horse needle? Maybe it hurts like hell and isn't registering thanks to their beautiful drugs?*

"Multiple shoulder fractures. Extensive soft tissue damage. We must run more tests. It's a surgery candidate."

Despite the drugs, Motorcycle Payback was making me nauseous. *I'll have to make the Bad News Update call.* The Road to Joy stops here, in a wheelchair.

He wasn't finished. More data on the clipboard. "Multiple hip fractures. Severe bruising. Vital organs in that area. No obvious signs of organ damage or internal bleeding, but we'll need to monitor."

A bullet dodged.

"Can't rule out head or spinal injuries. CT and MRI scans will be necessary."

When you're in a stupor, bad news is still bad

news, but it doesn't hit you over the head the way it should. Instead, it flares up and then sort of tickles you around the back of the head before sticking an uncomfortable finger in your ear.

"I'm afraid you've got a few months of recovery followed by a year of rehab in front of you. The orthopedic surgeon will see you tomorrow morning. We'll schedule surgery and transfer you to regional."

I don't know where it came from. It just slipped out. "I want to go home." It squeaked out in a weak, wee lad voice. *I want my mom! At least my bonus moms. "Have it done there."*

The doctor explained. "Potentially serious medical complications" and repeated the word "peril" several times. He sounded like the risk lawyers I'd worked with—I'm familiar with the routine. The lecture bounced off of me like water off a carnival duck's back. I was immune. Hardened. Didn't buy a word.

"Pretty sure I can make it home," I said calmly, trying to appear rational and execute a rapidly unfolding escape plan, based on sound logic: I have a good leg—Lenny gets around fine with one; what do I need my left arm and shoulder for? I'm right-handed! Get over the border into the arms of the government healthcare system I'd paid into for decades. Beats the hell out of going with the flow, away from home, ending up bankrupt, and living in a moldy rat-infested trailer on the outskirts of town. Rely on an unread *el cheapo* emergency travel insurance policy? I refused to throw up my arms, roll the dice, and end up condemned to a motorcycle-less life—a life without JOY. In the

collision between healthcare and insurance compan-
ies, the patient always loses. Insurance giants make
money by denying claims, not by paying out. That's
the point of fine print and litigation departments. I'd
heard lots of stories. *I want to go home! To have peace
of mind, not be bent by your wonderful drugs with Kathy
Bates waiting eagerly at the regional hospital.*

The doctor wasn't impressed. He wore his, *I'm the
expert here and know what's best, biker dude,* professional frown. The nurses seemed shocked that leaving
was even up for consideration. They were used to impact injury patients throwing in the towel. "There are
serious medical risks." The doctor repeated and ran
through several of them as if I was one of the thick
ones, incapable of absorbing the message. "A compli-
cation would be serious. Time is not your friend. The
sooner bones are set, the better the chance of success."

*Yeah, and the sky could fall, or a box jellyfish could
sting me in the ass.* I'd moved into competition mode.
Can't be done? Just watch me!

Conrad was back and taking Ferry Memorial's side.
"Stay put. Do as you're told!" Then he cheated and
phoned his wife, an ex-operating room nurse. An im-
partial expert, Joanne put her foot down. "Are you
nuts?" That advice rattled me. Maybe I am nuts? *She's
an expert. Knows so much more than me. Perhaps I
should pay attention?*

Left brain chimed in: Joanne can't see the billing
meter; she's used to universal socialized medical care,
not dealing with collection agencies and insurance
adjusters. Doesn't comprehend medical economics.

Doesn't realize insurance lawyers are already scanning my el cheapo policy, debating which loophole to destroy me with. *We'll teach those biker-idiots not to abuse the industry!*

Forget Joanne's advice, Left and Right Brain agreed. Lean hard into the curve and accelerate out. Don't become a patsy! Time to,

Scrape Your Pegs!

Words drifted around the room. "Blood clot. Trauma. Stroke. Brain bleed. Bones not setting. Organ failure. Time is critical." I wasn't listening. The song, Die Try'in drowned the doctor out.

I was thinking, if I stay, I'll have to make the follow-up Hospital Call. "Well, I can't leave. They're planning to slice me. Better check with the real estate agent. See what the house is worth. And check to see if there are any moldy rat-infested trailers for sale on the edge of town." Making the *I'm Out of the Hospital Call* was a better option.

As for Conrad, if you're in Emergency, with a person jettisoned off a motorbike and busted up, what are you going to say? Sounds like a smart plan, buddy. Let's get you the hell out of here. Ignore the medical experts. What do they know?

I convinced the doctor to give me a chance. Allow me to stand and demonstrate my one-legged mobility. I didn't mention I had Lenny Mobility Knowledge. *Not going to Mongolia, just across the border doc. Not planning to walk home.* Doctors, like motorcycle mechanics, aren't used to patients questioning their advice. So, I tried to express appreciation—never piss your mechanic or doctor off.

I figured I could drive a rental with one good arm and leg but was clever enough not to divulge that idea. There is probably a law about operating a vehicle while compromised and swallowing mind-numbing drugs. Never show your cards when you're planning an escape! I'd watched *Prison Break* and *Escape from Devil's Island.*

My left ankle was the size of a melon. My calf muscle had gone the opposite direction, shriveled, and in hiding. Parts of my leg were a disinfectant orange color. *Elephant Man, at least Elephant Man's left side.* The sight of it was demoralizing. *Escape? Dragging this horrific body with me.*

When I prepped and positioned for my attempt, an orderly provided a pair of tall crutches.

"Absolutely no weight on your left leg," the doctor instructed. He didn't need to; the slightest pressure triggered white-hot pain daggers and a foul bile taste that made me want to puke and pass out. A couple of warning blasts and everything I had at my disposal was focused on, "Absolutely no weight on my left side."

My left side didn't work except for my knee, which swung like a rusty hinge under my hospital dress, just enough to keep my cast boot off the floor as instructed. *See?* I looked proudly at the staff after. *Look at me, holding my leg off the floor, all by myself!*

Carefully, I placed a support stick under my left shoulder, as instructed by the doctor who had warned, "May not be possible." He was right. Now what? The doctor didn't look surprised. He wore an, I told you so dude, expression. You're not going anywhere.

Without a word, I switched the crutch to my right shoulder and attempted to hobble sideways rather than forward, keeping all weight off my left side, alternating between the crutch and right leg.

I started to topple. BC Nurse and an orderly rescued me. It sank in. I'm fucked up and not a Lenny. Carefully they lowered me back into the wheelchair. *Your goose is cooked, buster.*

I can't imagine what wounded battlefield soldiers must feel. Especially ones drafted and forced to participate in a farce. Shot to hell thanks to political science. No hope of survival unless the victims rescue themselves. Drag their maimed Elephant Man bodies home. Lie and die, or start crawling.

"Ready to try again," I declared.

BULLHEADED

The task: move the body with available resources, an inch at a time. Forward and to the right, with extreme caution. Backward and left impossible, but are unnecessary movements in a pared-down existence. Forward and right will get you where you need to go. An inch at a time. All concentration focused on the task at hand.

Up against my determination, the doctor had no option but to relent. Ferry Memorial is a hospital, not a prison. America the land of the free and I asserted my right to scrape my pegs.

An administrator arrived with a release on a clipboard. A ten pager. I signed and initialed, acknowledging my decision was contrary to Ferry Memorial's advice. I committed to having surgery within three days. Three days, four days, five days. Does it really matter? It's like manufacturers' maintenance intervals. They're designed for the worst-case scenario, with a generous fudge factor added on top of that. Tons of leeway. Same with bone intervals, I'm sure. Well, not one hundred percent, given I possess zero orthopedic knowledge and am a former fainter, but pretty sure it might follow logic similar to vehicle maintenance schedules.

It's nonsensical of the medical industry to pump patients full of drugs, then ask them to read and understand a ten pager.

Everyone, including Conrad, registered their disagreement, but it is MY body and MY future on the line. I'm a motorcyclist. I give laws, norms, and medical advice the finger! *Rebel Without a Cause,* but I had a cause, escape, then make it home. As for Conrad, he's ex-military. Everyone knows members of the armed services swear an oath to *no man left behind.*

I sat in a borrowed wheelchair in my flimsy gown with my supplies: pills, prescriptions, urine bottle, ice packs, and other medical stuff. There is only one taxi in Republic, Washington, and it wasn't taking calls. I'd checked myself out of the hospital but couldn't go anywhere.

I arranged my hospital blanket for modesty, pulling it over my dress. My brain functioned but like sludge, that's the way it is in Blobland. Still, I was not too bullheaded to understand: when the vote is many to one, you're probably wrong. Oh well.

I did nothing but wait, knowing Conrad would rectify the problem. He's good at that. In a nutshell, that was my escape plan—Conrad will sort things out. Even if I was firing on all cylinders, not visiting the outer limits, I'd have left it with Conrad. My solution would probably be no solution at all. "Let's pull my wheelchair with your GT. Only a mile to the motel." To make it sound sensible, I'd add, "Go easy on the gas!"

Conrad sorted it out.

BC Nurse drove me in her car to the motel; thank God for geographic bonding!

Conrad wheeled me into the motel handicap room. The chambermaid was leaving. She smiled as if we shared a connection, both fucked-up. Crystal meth, Skittles eating, chambermaid freak. I already missed my angels of mercy. *Want to see my pivot transfer? Onto the bed.*

Conrad had a room a couple of doors down. It was well past dinner time, he'd scout for supper downtown, a block away. "Maybe soup or yogurt." I hadn't eaten a thing besides some cherries and one pastry, but, in Blobland, there is no appetite. I mentioned "soup or yogurt" so Conrad would feel better. Provide a sense of normality. I was dependent on him to sort things out.

"TV," Conrad asked?

I shook my head, no. I had calm drugs, not cartoon-watching drugs. Dim light Blobland drugs.

Conrad left in search of food. I lay on the first of two queen beds. Flat on my back. Immobile. Boot cast, "not to be taken off." A lone wolf biker, now totally dependent. With a hospital urine bottle. Leg always elevated. Ice bag alternating between shoulder and hip. Scared that I had become a lesser being. Grim reality sinks in when you're alone, in a dimly lit handicap room, thanks to a motorcycle. Doubting it was worth it. Where's the joy now?

When the lights went out, on night one of my escape, thank God for opioids.

GOING DOWN

Sometime after midnight, I went down. It wasn't the ghost of Horace the Horrible; it was my fucked up, Elephant Man body.

I'd woken under the hospital blanket, in my dress, flat on my back, leg still in the air, drugs on low. I popped more pills, but in the minutes before serenity arrived, Fear No Evil yelled at me, "Get your ass off this bed! If you must, pee in the urine bottle, then inch your way to the sink. Do what normal people do! Brush your teeth. Wash your face. Take control! Are you going to lie on beds and wither away? Give up? Only twenty-five feet to the god damn sink. How hard can it be? Or stay and become crystal meth, Skittles eating junkie ex-biker freak. Your choice.

I swung my right leg off the bed and onto the floor. Pushed myself up. Half a pivot. Even though I was in a handicap room, there wasn't enough space to maneuver my wheelchair without assistance. So, I inched forward between the beds and the wall, using a leaning stick and the bed as a safety net. It was frightening; very unsteady, with a sink a marathon away. *How can you escape if you can't even make it to the bloody sink? Get on with it!*

I wanted to lie down, wait for the drugs to tell me, why bother? Blobland isn't so bad. But reaching the sink was a test not to be denied. My future depended on teeth brushing. I made it as far as the second bed before my body started to shake like an out-of-control washing machine. I tried to regain balance with the doctor's words ringing in my ear, "Put weight on your left side, and you'll coming back in an ambulance." When I twisted to help gravity, I dropped my leaning stick and crashed, terrified I wouldn't be getting up again on my own.

I lay on my right side, propped up by luggage, clenching my teeth. My phone, to be used to call Conrad if I needed anything, was on the bed table. I lay frozen at a thirty-degree angle, afraid of the damage report; *torpedoed again, captain. Bulkhead number four this time. Can't be sealed off. We're going down for sure!*

Skittle eating, crystal meth freak chambermaid would find me in the morning. Or Conrad? I didn't want him thinking, look at this guy. How pathetic is this? I'm going to sort this out by hauling his dumb ass back to Ferry Memorial. I'm ex-military, not a god damn nursemaid!

With all my weight on my right arm and leg, I slowly pushed and inched myself off the debris field until I was next to the second bed. It required everything I could muster, but eventually, I managed to retreat to the safety of my bed. I can't explain the difficulty. Lie down on the floor. Get up using one side of your body only. For the full effect, take some tranquil-izing drugs first. Then, allow an irate box jellyfish to sting your left side every thirty seconds.

Timidity and caution are essential lessons when you're a fragile ex-biker. No more damn the torpedoes.

Decrepit Rule #1: Not Being Cautious May Kill You!

On Monday morning, when Conrad arrived to kick off Day One operations, I was on the bed, in the com-pliant position. My three-day clock was ticking.

"Coffee," he asked?

"Sure." I smiled. My coffee addiction remained in-tact.

"Good rest?"

"Great." When will you have things sorted out?

COULD HAVE
BEEN WORSE

This question occurred to me: did speed make me lucky or unlucky? Could it have been worse? If I had been traveling faster, even two miles an hour faster, Horace and I would not have met on the highway. A speck of time can make an enormous difference. Correct, Professor Hawking?

Meth freak chambermaid dropped in to change the towels. When she asked, "How you do'in?" she seemed to understand my "could have been worse" answer. Probably in the same boat as me. A slight alternation in time, and she would have missed the first hit of drugs that trapped her.

Conrad returned from the U-Haul dealership, twenty miles from town, with bad news; they did not have a truck up to the job of loading two bikes, driver, and one decrepit for a trip to Victoria. Republic is a lovely town, but not when it comes to rental transportation. No airport either. Our faith was in the hands of U-Haul, and it was a bust.

I called Gigantic Insurance Company. Can you help? It's an emergency medical situation. "Exactly what my policy is all about," I explained. Need surgery within three days, but I'm stranded in a handicap motel room with a Skittles eating crystal meth freak chambermaid. I need emergency medical help! Who knows what will become of me on day four if you don't rescue me?

They took my information, entered it into their supercomputer, and told me to, "Hold on." The computer came back with, "Released from Hospital." It made no difference that I had escaped to attempt to reach a hospital where the insurance company would be off the hook. They had me. Checking myself out gave my insurer a big fat loophole, the one they chose to use against me. Section 9. Subsection 3. Clause 16. You get the picture: I was a victim of fine print. The fact that I was decrepit, required surgery, in pain, and was stranded and becoming demoralized, wasn't a consideration. They only considered hospital transfers "bed-to-bed." It was a limitation of their *el cheapo* policy. I threatened to return to Ferry Memorial to readmit myself, but there was provision for that as well; once you're out, you're out. That's it—there's no going back. Let's add an unofficial rule:

Always Read the Fine Print! Or ride with a contract lawyer without an intercom.

Experience is something you get just after you needed it, the saying goes. I'd torpedoed myself.

Now what? Here's a good thing to know about Conrad. He never said, "Told you so. Should have stayed put. You can be such a jackass." Didn't rub it in. If he says anything, it's with humor. Bob was like that. They'd have hit it off.

When all else fails, who bails you out? Family. I was lucky enough to have one. The family help desk doesn't have fine print. They had a brother prepped and on standby. On Day Two, Ron arrived in Republic to fetch his little brother.

PART 7: MORORCYCLE-LESS

FALLING BROTHERS

We grew up on the set of the Monty Python Lumberjack skit with a little Huckleberry Finn and Nancy Drew thrown in—fertile biker boy incubation ground.

My brother Ron toyed with motorcycles until Rule #1 nailed him in Montevideo, Uruguay, and he landed in a hospital for two months. Not a stone's throw away, like me. Instead of a deer, a car bumped his Korean scooter. New medical challenges layered on top of older injuries, ones predicted to prevent him from living, then walking, let alone riding a motorbike in South America decades later.

Compared to Ron's experiences, my deer encounter was a dream vacation. When he picked me up, I didn't expect, "Thank God, you're safe, little brother! Everyone's worried sick. Wheel over here! Let me give you a big fat hug." For Ron, my situation was a bump in the road, like being on the front line in Afghanistan; unless people are blown to smithereens, it doesn't register. Not a big deal. Carry on. *Are you going to get the free service dog?*

"Not so bad," I assured big brother #2 as I demonstrated my pivot transfer prowess and sat in his Tracker. The Tracker Ron pulled behind his colossal RV, now staged an hour north, in Grand Forks, BC.

Ron left the borrowed wheelchair at the motel office, cutting off my mobility lifeline. *Can I get to where I need to go, an inch at a time?* I was careful not to reveal signs of distress. Ron was watching. *Mustn't sob over the loss of a wheelchair.* If it were Barb or Joan, my bonus moms, the meetup would have been entirely different. But rather than a mom, the help desk sent the King of Bullheaded.

Skittle eating, crystal meth, chambermaid freak waved goodbye. I smiled and waved back. Surprisingly good customer service skills, I thought, for a meth freak. Maybe the tip I left by the TV helped? Probably a nice person, spit on by Life, the Bully. She was dealing with her own Horace the Horrible—hope she makes her escape and does well. I left a nice tip because it's admirable when people work at legitimate jobs to pay for their drugs, don't you think?

The Tracker backed out of its parking spot. "Escape in progress," I wanted to shout. Measured in feet, not inches. *We're off! Ron, sound the horn! Let's do a victory lap around Ferry Memorial!*

GT remained abandoned behind a sign on a fence that said, "Trespassers will be shot! Survivors will be shot again!" I felt bad.

At eleven AM, we were on the highway. Clear blue sky and brilliant sunshine; a fine day for traveling. Having gone through a traumatic event, you expect the world, at least the weather, would be on side—

gloomy and reflective. But it was the exact opposite. Upbeat, Life, the Beautiful weather. Perfect for Conrad. He would be in the Cascades, riding through the mountain pass, gorgeous scenery, sweeping curves, aiming to catch the afternoon state ferry home. Later, he told me he was "nervous as hell," his MRR cranked up. He used traffic as a shield. Constantly scanning for deer. "Scheduling worked out well, though. Right on time for the ferry." I missed him. And Bob.

I told Ron about my fall. I knew it was a pickup basketball game compared to the NBA final he'd starred in. Horrific to me, but benign to him. I wanted to wallow in accident pity like any respectable victim, but Ron isn't the guy. My accident was a day at the beach. I tried my best to make it sound like it could have been worse because the reality is, Ron knows it can be a hell of a lot worse.

When I was a youngster and Ron was barely twenty years old, Ron fell, well, not an actual fall—he was crushed. Not bashed by a road thanks to a deer, but pinned against a log by a yellowish, diesel fume belching, soulless Caterpillar. Where the hell was Buddha? Did he not ride in the circuitry of heavy equipment in the late nineteen sixties, Mr. Pirsig? You didn't mention in your stupid *Zen* book that the Big Man is selective. Two-wheel freedom machines only? No hitching rides on dozer tracks, crawling through mud, with hard-working loggers? No Zen and the Art of Heavy-Duty Mechanics? Is Buddha not comfortable submerged in grease?

Ron worked for Skeena Forest Products as a White-water Boom Man. Actually, he was a Whitewater Boom Boy (Skeena Forest Products didn't have a risk mitigation department). The mighty Skeena is a large, fast-flowing river in north western British Columbia, home of cedar trees capable of living a thousand years and growing up to 70m/230ft tall, unless a timber company knocked them down first, which is what Skeena River Forest Products was up to. The world had not yet done the math and figured out the sustainability equation. Tall, old-growth cedars were valuable commodities, not carbon cleaning giants.

Ron was the youngest on a crew of a dozen men, half of whom lived in a small logging camp nearby. The others, like Ron, commuted in a bus from town. My brother was born strong, athletic, stubborn, hard-playing, and hard working. He was made to be a Whitewater Boom Boy. Riding a motorcycle is child's play compared to riding a log down the Skeena River. He loved it. *Paid to ride? Are you kidding me?* The mere suggestion of such an occupation today would horrify regulators. I'm obstinate but may have to side with the *we're-here-to-protect-you* crowd on this one.

Ron led a small crew of older men that constructed booms, logs chained together in a backwater, to form a log corral. Timber, dumped into the Skeena upstream, would float down to be herded into a waiting trap. Three hundred logs to fill one boom. A river tug helped direct the careening missiles toward the opening. Along the river bank and in the backwater, Ron jumped from log to log with his peevee pole, a tool used to hook and move logs, push timber away from shore, break up jams, and direct the fallen trees into the boom. Like herding cattle into a chute, except on a fast-flowing, dangerous river. Once a boom was full, a tug would shepherd it toward a pulp mill or lumber mill forty miles away, at the edge of the Pacific Ocean.

 Ron loved the work. Riding booms was easy and natural for him. Not daunting, as it would be for a reasonable and cautious person. Not the hell of an office, or university campus, or the inside of a store. Had he been born in Wyoming; my brother would have been a cowboy. Enjoyed the Cowboy Breakfast at Rock Creek. Hung out with other cowpokes. Beat the shit out of anyone who needed a whoop'in. Rode a horse and stayed the hell away from heavy equipment and motorcycles.

Building booms requires skill, muscle, balance, and on-the-fly engineering. Different building techniques are used depending on the time of year and the water level. The boomsticks that make up the corral are secured together with chains. The ends of the logs that will form the opening rest on shore, tethered by cables, to secure the boom until it's time to position it in the river. Today's few remaining Whitewater Boom Persons are heavily clad in safety gear and regulations. In Ron's day, it was, *Just About Anything Goes.*

 A powerful bulldozer pulled the boomstick joints tight at the build site. The boom crew would lash the logs together with chains and then call the dozer to hook on and cinch outside sticks into place. At 2:20 on a sunny summer afternoon, Ron waved the Cat over. He jumped off a log to take the winch cable as he had done a hundred times before. His body was between a log and the dozer. WTF? Risk Mitigation Guy, where are you? My brother needs you! Stop writing up, Do Not Use This Power Tool While Bathing, and go where you're needed!

This time the bulldozer didn't stay put and wait for the command to move forward, to draw the boom-sticks tight. In a daze from the long hot summer work days, the driver reversed. By the time Ron realized what was about to happen, he was trapped (he admits to daydreaming about his girlfriend at the time). He screamed at the driver, but the Cat kept crawling back. He may have roared, "I don't want to die. Especially not like this! My girlfriend is waiting for me." I don't know? Ron only remembers feeling his bones break-ing. My antler nightmares don't compare to *bones-crushing-your-body-toward-death*. So, you see why I told my brother, "Could have been worse?"

A boom man threw his ax at the Cat, and the rescue began.

Early afternoon we pulled to a stop beside the big RV. Ron, the mobility expert, had a fix for my pathetic hobbling. "Forget the leaning sticks. Next to useless." Tucked away in a secret storage compartment was a pair of elbow crutches. A cuff goes around the forearm instead of under the shoulder. Hands latch on to horizontal grips. Elbow crutches distribute weight, relieving the shoulder.

Movement was still a struggle, but now I could manage inches at a time. I wondered why the medical experts never suggested elbow crutches? Part of their scheme to thwart my escape? Or was it a case of experience trumps medical college?

In front of the RV entrance were three foldable metal steps. No handrail. It may as well have been the Great Wall of China—an impossible barrier. Back in the Tracker, we drove to the community hospital, more a first aid and logistics center than a full-service hospital. My brother Lance, a year and a half older than me and a former member of the Royal Canadian Mounted Police, had called to give them an order: "Injured motorcyclist incoming. An escapee from the American billing system. Be prepared!" *If there's any trouble, I'll mount my horse and be there in a week!* Actually, Lance never rode horses or motorcycles, but he did fall over a waterfall.

Lance fell. FELL to be CRUSHED. Into a fast-flowing stream and then headfirst down a three hundred-foot / ninety-two-meter waterfall, like plunging off the top of Big Ben in London. He thought, no heavy equipment in this forest, what could go wrong? It was a beautiful day, like the day I met up with Horace. I had an appointment with a motel room. Lance had an appointment with a dot on a map.

He was an eighteen-year-old boy, working a summer job timber cruising in the Nass Valley, the process of mapping an area and measuring the volume and quality of standing and downed timber before it is harvested. It's now part of an indigenous tourist area. Some of the most beautiful scenery on Earth. It's the hereditary home of the Nisga'a people. There's a lava field, and a terrific motorcycle road—Conrad and I made the trek to Terrace to check the Nisga'a Highway out, a year before Horace. And visit one of my bonus moms and painter, Joan, and her family. On the drive, I had plenty of time to think about how one can be an artist and still be perfectly balanced, like Leonardo da Vinci. Joan and Leonardo could ride together. Horses or motorcycles. A moment of Absolute Clarity: of course, they could paint motorcycles on ceilings, as Michelangelo did on the Sistine Chapel. Pay homage to the Moses dirt bike! And touch-up Leo's Mona Lisa by adding a motorbike.

Years earlier, Lance and his twenty-year-old workmate, Rick, climbed out of a helicopter in a remote forest in north western British Columbia on a hot August morning. Young explorers. Dropped into the wilderness to join bears, mosquitoes, moose, and whatever nature had in store for them. No communication systems. No GPS. They were old-school explorers tramping through land man had never seen before —no mandatory safety compliance training. Mary, the receptionist at head office, was in charge of risk awareness.

The boy's objective: find a reasonable route to a predetermined dot on a topographical map. Plot the path on paper. Here's a compass and a chain to measure distance. Twelve miles to the dot. Better get a move on! In a later step, others would use their map, retrace their route to reach the dot, and inspect the value of the old-growth trees that stood waiting, their days numbered. Lumber and pulp mills have ravenous appetites.

Lance led, operating the compass. Rick followed, holding the far end of the measuring chain. Each compass reading translated into a visual landmark; usually a prominent tree used as a guide, toward the dot on the map. So, off they went, fixated on one landmark after another, never knowing what lay in their path until they covered the ground. At times, nature forced them to deviate off course, go around an impossible barrier before locking back on, taking a shot directly at the dot, always making a commotion to warn wild-life—stay the hell away from us! The only safety tip was: make lots of noise if you don't want to become bear food.

The boys encountered a fast-flowing stream in a shallow ravine on this August day. It stood between them and their next landmark. My brother stood in his heavy logging boots on rocks above the edge of the creek. I can jump back, he thought, away from the water. *After all, I was on the high school volleyball team. I know about jumping and keeping my eye on the ball.*

A boot slipped, and Lance was sliding toward the water. Hands still on the compass. His attention welded on the next landmark. He dismissed the thought of jumping backward. *Maybe a wet foot? Not so bad.* He eyed the opposite shore, but the rocks there were too steep and jagged to attempt a crossing. *A wet foot it is.*

Fast-flowing mountain water is deceptive. Streams look peaceful, flowing through undisturbed nature, but carry the massive power of an unstoppable force. Sir Isaac could calculate the energy, but imagine fifty fire hoses blasting you. A boot slipped into the stream. And then the other. There was no hope. The current was far too strong, and heavy gear weighted the boy down. The waterfall waited, a few car lengths downstream, its proximity determined by the route to the dot. A three-hundred-foot / ninety-two-meter plunge to certain death. *You boys should be home, fooling around with your girlfriends, not out here, tramping through my forest. Bag groceries if you must have a summer job! Or serve soft ice cream. What do you think you're doing here, on your own, eyeing my trees?* The current picked my brother up and flung him over the cliff. *Off with you! Be gone!* No Buddha. He was busy hanging out in Mr. Pirsig's old Honda at that time.

What awaited Lance was a horrific bombardment against rocky outcroppings before bleeding to death as water pinned him at the bottom of the falls.

His six-foot body dropped over the edge, and he nosedived toward his end of days. Faced with the shock and terror of what was about to happen, most people would black out, retreat to Blobland to shield their minds from the horror of what lay ahead, their brain matter hopelessly confused by the impossible situation. Life does not prepare you for plummeting down a waterfall.

Lance knew he was not going to survive if his body shot into whatever waited at the bottom of the falls. What to do? "Time kind of stood still. Life does flash before your eyes." Valley of Death, I thought, listening to my brother talk? He was definitely headed in that direction. "Memories" was the word he used. "They prompted me to want to save myself." Physically close to death, but mentally, Lance never conceded. In the river, I got a video. Lance got memories. Eerily similar. But maybe different? One a call to action. The other an acceptance. Each of us pushed by water toward our Valley of Death. Ron was beside the Skeena river. Death by water. Like Bob.

"You know how, when you're a kid, you think you can jump, just before you hit the ground to save yourself? It was sort of like that. I thought I could jump before I hit bottom to save myself... more maneuver than jump, but the same idea. I can save myself, I thought. I know it sounds silly, but I really did believe I would figure something out." Hopelessness and despair would have seized me, I'm sure. *I'm going to die, and I'm just a kid. How unfair is that? Mother of God, why me?* But Lance wasn't overcome. "I had time to think. It was surreal. As if it were happening in slow motion." The opposite of my collision on Highway 20. If you have the presence of mind, tumbling down a tall waterfall gives you time to think: *What can I do to prevent my imminent death?* Talk about a Newtonian moment! Exactly what can you do if you find yourself plummeting down a waterfall?

Scape Your pegs!

Lance glimpsed a rock ledge poking through the cascading water below him. He had dropped about 150' / 46m with at least another 100' / 30m to go. Somehow, he swung his body enough to aim his lumberjack "cork" boots at the ridge. His boots hit the outcropping, slowing his momentum. He spotted a second lower ledge to his right. One without sharp jagged edges, just out of reach. He forced his body to roll, moving it against the power of the water determined to push him down. His body moved far enough right to hit the second rock ledge, slamming into its surface. Rock rather than asphalt. Head against stone, like me, but without protection, aside from desperately flapping arms. The force of the water pushed Lance against the ledge until it pinned him, snagged on a rock, dangling beside a waterfall. Sounds awful, but, under the circumstances, it was a great place to be.

 Lance lost consciousness. No angels of mercy, but Rick was there, horrified. He raced toward a logging road through the bush while Lance

bled on the ledge. Eventually, a rescue team and a helicopter arrived.

By coincidence, a national TV crew was in Terrace doing a story. They diverted to Mills Memorial for the much better, Miracle Boy Survives Waterfall, story. Miracle Boy made the national newscast and other news groups picked up his story, and Lance got his minute of fame the hardest way possible. Unfortunately, no talking; his voice box, bruised from the fall, the Prince of Bullheaded was speechless for weeks.

At Grand Forks Hospital, they took more X rays, consulted with other hospitals, and agreed the best option for me was to be close to home, in a full-service hospital. On Wednesday, August 21, with assistance, I flew to Victoria and, at five o'clock on Day Three, wheeled into Royal Jubilee, a five hundred bed state-of-the-art hospital half an hour from home. An orthopedic surgeon operated on the following morning. Day Four, technically breaking the terms of my agreement with Ferry Memorial by a day.

I was the last brother to end up in the hospital, damaged. My oldest brother Dave began the parade when he broke his arm after falling from a rock cliff. I recovered in Royal Jubilee for two weeks, learning how to cope without the use of half of my body, the

Elephant Man half. My roommate was another bike accident victim. He'd hit a curb on his bicycle, toppled over, and broke his hip. So, I guess there's a Bicycle Lottery as well.

When you're in a hospital alone, uneasy, and motorcycle-less, you can't help but think, why me? The answer is: MOTORCYCLES.

AFTER THE FALL

There is a gradual progression from motorcycle to hospital bed, to wheelchair, to a mobility scooter, to crutches, walker, water-walking, cane, trekking poles, and slowly, building strength to learn what your limitations are likely to be. It's part of Motorcycle Payback. Remember Newton? Every force has an equal and opposite reaction? Motorcycle JOY has a price.

The best advice I received from doctors and therapists is worth repeating: people who have a positive attitude and work at recovering do well. People who become resigned, feel sorry for themselves, do little and quickly go downhill.

Another way of putting it—if you tell yourself, Good enough. Fuck it! You'll end up a permanent resident of Blobland. If you're stubborn, you're in the game. I didn't share family perseverance stories with my doctors and therapists. I could have said, "Listen to this," but I felt it might make my repair experts less enthralled with my progress. *Oh. You have examples? It's in your genes? That's much less impressive than recovering all on your own.*

My wife, Dori, looks after me while I do minuscule exercises in my room in the basement; the staircase bars my way to the main floor. I point my broken foot toward imaginary hour marks on a clock and shrug my busted shoulder. When trivial actions become your Mount Everest, you know it'll be a long slow climb to the summit. If you're stubborn, you repeat twice as often as instructed by your in-home therapist.

Our cat Bunny was my coach, and Pearl was my cheerleader.

ZEN AND THE ART OF MOTORCYCLE RIDING

Two months after my release from Royal Jubilee, Bob flew into the Thompson River. I'd been thinking about my falling brothers and how they handled their experiences. To add to that, now there was the question of what happened to Bob? As I recuperated and researched, the puzzle pieces formed a picture.

Bob had it figured out. There was more to my motorcycle friend than met the eye, but I'd never been able to put my finger on what it was. Now, on reflection, it seems obvious. When I joked about Buddha hitchhiking on his Multistrada, Bob explained, "It's conceptual. When you ride, you're connected."

"So?"

"Enlightenment is the interconnectedness of all things."

"So?"

He liked to joke about being a Transformer. The shift that happens *Before-Motorcycle* and *On-Motorcycle*. The constant swing between nothingness and awareness that can occur when you're riding. How the drone of the engine and the wind can make your mind think about nothing and then everything. Days and months of life happen in minutes and hours on-motorcycle. Riding is a quest, like life condensed in time. The perfect ride doesn't last long; life is like that. It changes. Always forward to the next event.

In our minds, Bob and I were hardened survivors. Curmudgeonly Jackasses. But we had the terminology wrong. Like my falling brothers, Bob processed a touch of Zen, the ability to deal with consequences. I just hadn't put an appropriate label on it.

I've said the Motorcycle Riding Rules are about **Ability** and **Awareness.** But it should be **Ability, Awareness, and Accountability**. The world is what it is; each rider must be accountable,. Bob knew. "You are in charge of your ride. Not Buddha."

Life hands you experience. Some of it makes sense. Other parts make you wonder? Why was Horace on Highway 20? Why did a bulldozer crush the King of Bullheaded? Push The Prince of Bullheaded over a waterfall and Dave off inanimate objects? Karma? The law of cause and consequence? When you ride, you can't stop the rain that pelts you for hours and eventually seeps into your skin no matter what you wear. Or the sun and heat that fry you like a battered pickle. But you can be skillful about the way you react.

Life handed my brothers horrible accidents. Who knows why? Let's not speculate on controlling cause.

Each brother responded with deep determination. They were skillful and accountable, taking responsibility for outcomes.

As a consequence of thinking, and with guidance from YouTube, I'm adding "Zen" to the way I define my life practice now. Sure, I'm a jackass and possibly a curmudgeon, but I am one who will consciously be accountable for consequences. Instead of cursing and Why Me's? it'll be What Next? The extent of my recovery and how I manage what I become is up to me. Think of yourself as a Zen Jackass, and the consequences will be better than being a Curmudgeonly Jackass, don't you agree? One paltry word. I feel better about myself already. Rebranded. A new and improved me.

I suspect Bob had the great ride of causality figured out. He never blamed; he dealt with consequences. If I suggested swapping "Curmudgeon" for "Zen." "Just a word," he'd say. I think. Probably, that's what he'd say. I wish to God he were here now to talk it through. To assure me, "yes, I knew all along. It has nothing to do with maintenance. Nothing whatsoever."

Bob owned two motorcycles; both were his sanctuary. He rode his cruiser to his grave. Or his next beginning? Reincarnated? They say he had pancreatic cancer. Who knows why Life, the Bully picked on my friend, but Bob dealt with his sentence. He scraped his pegs in the Thompson River.

RIDE AGAIN?

It's been months since Horace and I met up. The scene replays in my mind, sometimes in a nightmarish way. Other times, as a question, "What's next?" People ask, "Will you ride again?" If you can?

"Probably not," I answer when asked. It'd be crazy, right? My number would go back in the draw. Family members would ask, "Didn't you learn anything? One Hospital Call is enough!"

I have nothing but time on my hands. "Will I climb back on," is a question that eats up a lot of it? Bones mend. Memories diminish. Soft tissue pain dulls. I may be physically capable in a year, but will I be comfortable, in body and mind, on a motorcycle?

I admit to being fearful. Not so bullheaded. I read stories about riders who "got right back on the next week." "I climbed on with my cast." "Don't be a weenie! Get the fuck back on!" These are real bikers. True outlaws! Me, I'm a Zen Jackass or, as Marta says, "A jackass whose number came up." She's requested I transfer funds from the motorcycle travel budget to Snacks and Washroom Maintenance because "you won't be traveling much." Maybe. I enjoy the battered pickles more now that I can't ride to Wyoming for the Cowboy Breakfast.

I spend hours lying on my back browsing. "Maybe I'll find a Therapy Bike," I tell Bunny. "A machine that fits my new circumstances? Immune to Kamikaze deer. More recovery tool than a motorcycle." After many years, I miss not having a motorcycle resting in the garage. To talk things over with. The house seems empty without one. Being motorcycle-less makes me feel uneasy.

You'd think I'd hate motorcycles, but I don't. Bunny understands. There is more than one way to skin a cat, right Bunny?

Recovery is a tough slog. There are times you want to throw up your hands and be done with it. No! Be stubborn in a good way! Be accountable. At a minimum, healing must get me to where climbing on is my decision. I work at recovering; it's my job now that I'm a Zen Jackass.

Mostly, I don't want to concede to Marta. "I guess we could move all of your Travel Budget into Snacks and Washroom Maintenance." I know she's playing around with a reverse persuasion technique. "Won't be going far on that mobility scooter. Plus, you've been eating an awful lot of battered pickles."

To add to the excitement, a pandemic is attacking the world, scaring the shit out of people, including my rehabilitation services. The good news is, I'm sticking with Zen Jackass-ism. I refuse to say, *Good enough. Fuck it! Fuck you COVID-19!*

I'm carrying on, on my own, in my own way.

So is Marta. She's making pickles—The World's Battered and in a Pickle, Pickles.

KICKSTANDS UP, MY FRIENDS.

I'll report back on my next stop, in *The Joy of Motorcycle, More Scraping Pegs*, thanks for riding with me.

APPENDIX

APPENDIX A
– RULES

Ten Motorcycle Riding Rules:

#1. Everyone is trying to kill you!
#2. Don't Kill Yourself by Doing Something Stupid!
#3. Ignoring Motorcycle Physics May Kill You.
#4. Your Motorcycle May Be Trying to Kill You!
#5. Complacency Can Kill You.
#6. Your Own Noggin is Trying to Save You.
#7. Be Stubborn in A Good Way.
#8. Your Number May Come Up.
#9. Irritants May Get Your Goat.
#10. The Multiplier Effect is Also Trying to Kill You!

"Hope Rule #11 doesn't sink us," Marta says referring to the rule in development to be introduced in *The Joy of Motorcycles, More Scraping Pegs*. Ten is the correct number for a list, according to my advisor.

APPENDIX B
– VALVES

Zen and the Art of Motorcycle Maintenance, maintenance.

VALVE ADJUSTMENT:

1. Go to YouTube
2. Search for your bike's How-to Adjust Valves videos.
3. Turn YouTube off.
4. If your bike has a valve adjustment symptom like pre-ignition or overheating, go to #6.
5. If your bike has no symptoms and is running fine, get a second opinion from Buddha before blowing your money.
6. Take your bike and your credit card to Service.

THANKS & LINKS

Enjoyed the book? Please consider leaving a review.
Thanks!

Scraping Pegs & Email
https://beatenstickpress.wixsite.com/mysite

Scraping Pegs on Facebook

ACKNOWLEDGEMENT

Editor: Mark Gint

Proof: Helen Joan Brady

My Angels of Mercy: Washington Emergencey Services, Ferry Memorial Hospital, Royal Jubilee Hospital, the Stewart Family Help Desk.

The Copley Park Dog Moms

Dori, Colin & Monica (Pearl & Bunny)

Conrad Moller

BOOKS BY THIS AUTHOR

Scraping Pegs, The Truth About Motorcycles

Ten Motorcycle Riding Rules and meeting Horace the Horrible.

The Joy Of Mototcycles, More Scraping Pegs

An inquiry into JOY and recovering from Horace the Horrible.

Printed in Great Britain
by Amazon

10157368R00140